QUICK! BEFORE THE
MEMORY FADES

D1513686

QUICK! BEFORE THE MEMORY FADES

by

NANCY REID

Printed and published by
Highland Printers Ltd.,
Diriebught Road, Inverness, Scotland

First Printed 1975

CONTENTS

Contents — *continued*

INTRODUCTION

The hills and glens of the Highlands have felt the marching of men since pre-history — the people who carved the Boarstone, those who put up the stones at Clava, the ever-warring Clans, the punitive red-coats, the labourers who put the Canal through the Great Glen, those who put the railways through . . . countless men.

The march of the electricity pylons is less noisy but they have changed the Highlands as nothing in history did.

This was a unique area remote from cities with a culture all its own. Electricity took the force and the splendour from the water-falls. It sent the pylons marching over the landscape; it brought light at the touch of a switch; and many boons to the housewife, the farmer, the crofter.

It took away the sense of separateness. It brought a window on the world into the living room and made children question the beliefs of generations dividing the generations more harshly than in more populated areas.

In the last few years industry has come to the Highlands bringing an influx of people from other areas of the British Isles and from other countries. The incomers seem to be overwhelming the people who belong to the Highlands.

The Highlanders are the most hospitable of people, having welcomed to their hearths generations of Service men and regularly entertaining Transatlantic cousins who come for the charter flight three weeks.

It is not surprising that it seems that the traditions and culture — the way of life founded on values particularly Highland — is being eroded by a tide of incomers greater than ever before in history.

The inspiration of this book is to set down memories of the old days of separateness to the delight of old and young today and the generations to come.

Readers of the Nancy Reid Page in the Highland News Group of Newspapers have sent us their memories and enjoyed recalling them. Here they are for you to read, with some of the legends which were handed down by story-tellers in the old days. I have left them just as I received them — as first-person narratives — for that is the authenticity.

It is a book to read right through, if you wish, or to dip into as a bedside book. It is a book which I am sure will fascinate; which will be read again and again; and which will bring back their home-land to the Highland families in the four corners of the earth.

Read it against a background of living memory of the hard life on a croft where families were brought up, strong and well-educated, on food which they produced themselves — milk, eggs, butter, cheese, oats, potatoes and other root vegetables—and the village school.

Picture a time when a shepherd worked without dogs, the sheep following him in a Biblical skein at his heels.

Picture Farraline Park, Inverness, without the buses and car park. The crumbling classical building recently vacated by the Police was a school, which men in prominent positions in the town today, attended as boys. Picture the soldiers drilling in that wide flat area.

Imagine the doctor's family in a lovely house with large garden, sharing a wall with the foundry in Academy Street. They kept four dogs which never needed to be taken for walks. They roamed the streets of the town in safety and enjoyed the large garden.

Imagine a man going to work one day in the 1880s and catching a hare in lower Church Street, Inverness.

Imagine the people of quality converging on the Northern Meeting Rooms in Church Street in exquisite dresses and impeccable male evening dress for the Ball on summer evenings before the Wars.

Imagine the buyer from an Inverness fashion house going to Paris to do her buying.

Imagine? Many of the readers of this book will not have to imagine. The stories bring back the golden reality of memories in summers when the sun always shone and winters when the snow laid a mantle over everything and there was skating by lantern light on Loch na Sanais and the doctor made his rounds by sleigh.

NANCY REID.

LOCHARDIL,
INVERNESS.

What the lady motorist wore in 1903. On the left: Baltic silver-grey seal coat with collar and revers of skunk. On the right: Harris tweed three-quarter length lined with reindeer skin.

A

Name	Overtime			£	s	d
R. L. Grant				1	17	6
J. Mackintosh				1	10	"
J. Watt	"	"	8	1	6	8
J. Simpson				1	6	"
J. Rose				1	6	"
G. Dorward				1	6	"
A. Dickie	"	1	"	1	7	"
A. Ritchie	"	1	"	1	7	"
R. Duncan				1	6	"
J. Giles				.	18	"
K. Mackenzie				"	18	.
R. Jenkins	"	1	4	.	17	4
R. Jeans	.	1	8	"	15	8
G. Phimister	"			"	3	6
P. Macleod				"	3	6
A. Fraser (1)				"	3	6
W. Jenkins				"	3	6
D. Bisset	"	2	"	1	12	"
A. Robertson				"	17	"
W. Wilson				"	3	6
A. Fraser (2)				"	3	6

Foreman's time and pay book for a Highland printing house in 1881. Total wage bill for the Composing and Machine rooms for the week illustrated was £19 11s 2d including overtime. Adults averaged around £1 6s per week.

Teaching in
the Thirties

MY FIRST permanent teaching post was in a rural school with a roll of 34 children whose ages ranged from 14 to 5 years. I was in sole charge and had to teach everything from algebra to the alphabet in one large room. I was young and enthusiastic but found that the older boys regarded me more as a girl to be wooed rather than as a class teacher. Fortunately I was engaged and my would-be admirers had a healthy respect for the officer of the law whose ring I wore.

Jockie arrived to be enrolled in October as he and the rest of the tinker fraternity had come to roost for the winter months in the far north after wandering over the Highlands during spring and summer. His winter home was a small brown tent in a disused quarry a stone's throw from the school and was so low that it had to be entered igloo-fashion. Jockie's family consisted of Jacob, the father; Rebecca, the mother; Sarah, the daughter; and Benny the baby (13 other children had died in infancy). Jockie's age was uncertain and his mother had no idea of his birth-date. He looked like a Neander-thal man: short; stocky; long, gangling arms; hunched shoulders; black, snake-like eyes; dark hair and skin; and dressed in long trousers, torn, wide and unhemmed and held up halter-wise with a rope which was tied round his neck. His big shoes made a shuffling noise; every toe was exposed; and there were no laces for support to his wide, splayed feet. His jacket would have fitted a well-known Liberal M.P. and he had a sly, furtive look on his face, like an animal that had been maltreated, starved and beaten.

Jockie's first lessons consisted of copying his name, learning sounds and letters and matching symbols with numbers, but it was a very difficult job, like denying a falcon the right to fly as Jockie was Nature's child with the call of the wild inherent in his blood. I think he deliberately decided to make no progress, as when I asked him to add two and two he always said "64. Miss," He was in present-day

1

parlance uneducable but, considering his deprivations and background, what chance had he of attainment in any educational subject?

In those days there were no school dinners and young children of five years walked to school for six miles in all weather conditions. I boiled a kettle the size of a witch's cauldron on the hob of an open fire and there it simmered until lunch time and I made the cocoa with the help of the older pupils. Jockie's lunch was a hunk of dry, stale bread as hard as the Barren Rocks of Aden; and to supplement this prisoner-like diet I used to give him my left-over sandwiches which he wolfed down and so established between us a kind of entente cordiale.

One morning, Jockie was absent but before lunch came a knock at the class room door. Mother Rebecca and Jockie. They had been to a nearby town on foot and on the four-mile walk back Jockie had an accident. Coming up the very narrow road that led to the school a farm-labourer on a bicycle had run over Jockie's foot, bursting open his big toe. I was asked to give medical attention. Leaving my class I filled a basin with hot water (from the simmering kettle), poured half a bottle of disinfectant into it and immersed Jockie's foot into it. Not a whimper from his lips. Then from the medical box I lavished some ointment on a bandage and dressed the toe. As Jockie was barefooted I wrapped two yellow dusters round the foot and secured them with safety pins, instructing Rebecca to go to the local Post Office and get the postmaster to phone for the District Nurse as I was sure that blood poisoning would follow from my makeshift attentions. A few days later I met Jockie, still with yellow dusters intact on his injured foot, and plus severe scratches on the backs of both hands, got as he jauntily told me, from trying to catch a weasel.

Now the cocoa developed a distinctly unpleasant taste and I decided to suspend serving it at lunch time until I could contact the appropriate authority and find out the cause. This took some time and irate parents were displeased at their children not having their mid-day hot drink. The firm responsible for laying the pipes for school water supply found that there was a seepage from a cow's byre that was finding its way into the water supply, hence the weird-tasting cocoa! I marvelled that there were no outbreaks of sickness among my pupils. They were apparently impervious to ills that could have caused a serious infection among children who were less healthy, tough and hardy.

On returning after the Easter holidays in 1938 I saw two large caravans parked, by permission of the Education Authority, in the school playground. Their occupants were three Germans: a Professor Wolfgang, his wife and secretary, the latter bearing a striking likeness to Goebbels, Hitler's propaganda minister. They were to be there for six to eight weeks and their ostensible object was to photograph and measure the physical characteristics of the tinkers. In hindsight, we now know that this seeming interest in the tinkers was a clever excuse to survey the land and take notes on nearby harbours and other geographical features.

The Professor and his wife were typically Aryan, tall, angular and blonde; while Goebbels' double was small and obsequious. The trouble began when the Professor and his aides tried to interview the tinkers and became self-constituted Torquemadas. The tinkers would have no dealings with the Germans, as some of them were veterans of World War One. One of them produced an old rifle and threatened the Germans with grievous bodily harm if they didn't go back to the Fatherland.

Wolfgang immediately went to the police and asked for protection against threatening behaviour, non-co-operation and illegal use of fire-arms. It was surely ironic that a police car escorted these Germans to every tinker camp and the tinkers complied, under duress, to have their photos taken, skulls measured, families indexed, all for sixpence as payment for their compliance.

However, one septuagenarian named Charlotte was not deceived. She met me one morning on the way to school and said "Miss, they are spies. Will you tell the police? Nobody will listen to us and if we don't co-operate they will charge us with poaching or frame us in another way." Charlotte then told me that the Germans had hidden maps and papers inside the inner tubes of their tyres and were always asking questions about the tides in the Firth and other matters concerning the county. I passed on Charlotte's suspicions to the police, but they laughed and said she was always drunk as well as being senile and who would believe such lazy, shiftless vagabonds?

After leaving the North the Germans crossed the sea to Norway and there, no doubt, were received as genuine travellers seeking knowledge to file away for future use. In September, 1939, war was declared on Germany and poor old despised, illiterate, Charlotte proved to be more visionary, fey and prophetic than all the politicians, police and pundits who scorned the warnings of an old tinker as the ravings of an unlettered dotard.

3

I look back in sorrow and deep anger at the appalling, degrading conditions of Jockie's childhood and the utter indifference of Church and State. No one tried to alleviate the miseries of these unfortunate wanderers in their own country. Jockie suffered from malnutrition, brutality and complete deprivation of even the bare necessities of life. My most vivid memory of him today is when he tried to clean his nose with a handful of frog spawn concealed in his pocket. He could never keep the rags I constantly doled out to him for this purpose.

Tinkers were usually looked upon as undisciplined unprincipled rogues, but I look back with affection and nostalgia at the days of my youth and my tinker children, who believe me, were well behaved and knowledgeable in the ways of birds and small animals. There was, however, something primeval and engaging about them.

I know that Jockie has spent the greater part of his life in prison for unsocial behaviour, and who can wonder? No sheriff's warning, internment or rehabilitation can ever undo the neglect, indifference, misery, cruelty and deprivation suffered by this Oliver Twist who unlike his earlier counterpart, can have no promising future because of the dark, brutal childhood spent in a wretched, primitive tent in a wet, disused quarry.

I don't know how old he is now, but I hope he can remember to write his name as I taught him so that he can secure some of the pecuniary and other benefits which were so utterly denied to him in his childhood and youth, and that society won't judge him too harshly for his all too frequent misbehaviour.

Hog Money Night and Rent Day

TWO notable dates in the crofter's calendar were Hog Money Night and Rent Day. In the Corpach district, the Laird, Cameron of Lochiel, held the right to rent the crofts from November to March. For this right he paid out Hog Money for grazing his winter hogs.

Came the night. Bush telegraph summoned the crofters. The local Clerk-cum-Treasurer drew the amount required the day before, when it was specially deposited in the Bank by the Laird. The money was allocated according to the number of cows per head. This sum varied from year to year and the sum received by each person was more often taken with a grouse than a smile.

Deductions for bull upkeep, shepherds' pay, etc., were very unpopular. The largest whack went to the parish minister for the Glebe — where no hogs were grazed. On one occasion the district councillor was so annoyed he withheld the cash — but peremptorily had to fork out. The minister had no scruples about enforcement of the law. The shepherd paid a man £1 for the season. This was to cut down all briar bushes, bramble bushes, etc., that tore wool off the hog's back.

Next event: Rent Day. This found the crofters foregathered in the local hotel to pay their rents — about equivalent to the money that had been paid out. The Laird got his money back and all seemed satisfied with the bargain . . . and Lochiel's dram!

On the fringe of these memorable Day and Night proceedings, some heated arguments took place. Drams loosened tongues. Crofting laws were amended or made anew. One law-knowing wife withheld her rent on the ground that it was illegal to pay it in an hotel.

For every cow on the croft a stook of corn (12 sheaves) had to be supplied for winter-feeding the bull. Sheaves were weighed, and if underweight, extra sheaves had to be added. In summertime the bull had to be herded by a crofter for so many days. This was a constant source of grievance, for a bull could batter down fences and gates. One crofter solved the problem by acquiring a herd of cows. He was happy to herd the bull.

All those old days and customs. Like most of the folk who lived in them and with them, they have passed away. They remain vivid only in the minds of old stagers like me.

How many old stagers up in Caithness remember "carvey biskads" — biscuits liberally sprinkled with sugar-coated carroway seeds? A correspondent recalling those delicacies also recalls: "Jessie Mowat's mouth-watering meat pies; from the wee shoppie in Swanson Street; Mrs Norn's cream cookies with real, fresh cream; and the baker who used to trundle his barrow around the riverside area selling his goods." Personal service indeed,!

Sandy was a kenspeckle figure

HALF-A-CENTURY ago the Highlands had men and women who were regarded as "characters." They were outspoken people who never hesitated to air their views in public about various subjects and people. Such a person was old Sandy, a kenspeckle figure in our glen.

He had soldiered in far-away countries; ooh! the tales he could tell to the children who listened to them with bated breath and hung on to his every word as though they were precious jewels falling from his lips. If stories were slightly exaggerated, as they sometimes were, how were the bairns to know? To them Sandy's stories were as true as those in the Bible.

He loved his garden and the children, especially the boys, delighted in helping him. Sandy's garden held far more attraction for them than did Dad's, but then Dad couldn't tell such good stories about monkeys, lions and elephants! Fishing was Sandy's second love, and many a boy played truant to escort him up the glen to the burns, and on occasion, to the loch. He was a kind-hearted man who liked to share his "catches" with his neighbours; so that we all enjoyed fresh trout for breakfast, or fried pike for tea.

He excelled at handiwork, so was a grand help for me in keeping the bairns interested and amused. He could fashion the most life-like hares, rabbits and deer I've ever seen out of wood and plasticine. He had a great contempt for money, and certainly looked upon it as the root of all evil. In his youth he had had a sweetheart whom he once described to me. Of her he said "Her cheeks were like roses, her skin white as milk, and her eyes like bluebells dancing in the wind." Looking up at me he went on "Aye! And her hair was like your own: blue-black and glossy as a raven's wing." "Did she die, Sandy?" I asked sympathetically. "No," he said, "she threw me

7

over for a rich man and oh! how I've ever since hated the filthy lucre!"

Sandy had a wealthy cousin in Australia who sometimes sent him parcels of food and clothing. His eyesight was failing and this cousin had promised to send Sandy a pair of eye-glasses in the next parcel; but as week followed week and no parcel arrived Sandy was naturally a little downhearted. He remarked to me one day "Well, many's the time when I was a boy at school did I write in my copy book that hope deferred maketh the heart sick, but I never understood what it really meant till now." Neither did I, and my heart bled for Sandy.

Next day I said to the children "We must help Sandy" so we put our heads together and made a pair of spectacles out of snare wire and celluloid paper. True, they weren't very substantial. We wrapped them in tissue paper, put them into a cardboard box, tied it up with brown paper and string and affixed a stamp. On top of it I drew a postmark in black ink which I then carefully obliterated. Calling on him after school hours I said "What box is this the postie has left on your table, Sandy?" It was pathetic to see the old man's joy. The specs were tried on and much admired. He declared he could see fine with them and to prove it picked up a newspaper and began to read.

The spectacles didn't stand up very long to Sandy's absent-mindedness, and he said to me one day, "No wonder I never went to Australia, with the poor workmanship that is out there. They don't even know how to put right glass in glasses!"

The Templars
did everything

I.O.G.T. did not mean — "I owe Granny tuppence", as the school bairns used to say. It was Independent Order of Good Templars, an organisation which had a strong following in the North.

The members of this body were pledged to total abstinence from intoxicating liquor. There were two Lodges in Thurso — St. George's, which met in Grove Lane, and Shamrock, whose meeting place was behind Tollemache House.

St. George's Lodge had a junior section which was always well attended.

Hugh Dunwoodie, and subsequently, the late Cristina Miller, were the Superintendents during these years.

"Beely" Sinclair was the hall-keeper and these people gave sterling service to the many and varied functions carried out in the Templar's Hall.

There were impromptu concerts during the children's meetings and much coaxing was required to get some of the children on to the stage. Then it was difficult to get them off! How many of us made our debut on the stage of that hall? Who can forget the haunting melodies of Phemie and her accordion?

The Lodges combined on New Year's Day in organising a carnival. This consisted of competition stalls — lucky dips, roll-the-penny, guessing the model train stops, raffles, horse-racing (one had to jerk a model horse along a string. More often than not, one's "horsie" toppled over!)

There was rifle-shooting for the youths and coconut shies — the targets being canvas heads stuffed with sawdust and bearing the

9

names of local celebrities. The voluntary work done by the Templars in organising and running entertainments in Thurso was first-class and the Temperance Hall was the venue of a great variety of entertainments, including films, concerts, boxing and dances.

Shamrock Lodge, of which I was a member for many years, held their meetings on Wednesdays and the majority of us visited St. George's on Friday evening, which was their meeting night.

Ex-members will remember the enjoyable evenings we spent. After business we held small social gatherings — dances, parties, quiz sessions, "Tail the Donkey" and even "Postman's Knock." How we loved the opportunity of getting a certain staid old maid outside, during "Postman's Knock" and delaying her return to the hall. She'd be fuming ("What will people be thinkan?)" much to the delight of our pals.

Another of our special evenings was "Pound Night". Each member had to take along 1lb. of some useful household commodity. "Yours truly" and his pals always took a pound of coarse salt — this was the cheapest, and cost only a penny!

These articles were auctioned to the members. The late Mr W. Brotchie was Chief Templar, ably supported by Bob Simpson, who, with other office-bearers, had a difficult job trying to control the exuberance of our youth!

I remember being appointed a delegate, along with one of my pals, to a special meeting in Bower. We found that there were more and better attractions in Bower than meetings! Our report the following week consisted of a few words "A good time was had by all". I may add that that was the last opportunity we had of visiting a sister Lodge in an official capacity.

As previously mentioned, the hall of St. George's was used for many functions. One was the Swifts Ball, an annual event which had a large support. Another very popular annual promotion was the Fish-Workers' Ball. My memories of these are limited — just a "teet-in" at the windows and taking note of the intricacies of the Charleston. What a pity these are nothing but memories.

The war years of 1939-45 seemed to change the pattern of life in Thurso. Some people blamed the T.V. and others said "We're gettan owld" One is as old as one feels! I am sure some of us old 'uns could show the young ones how to trip through the Lancers or an Eightsome reel.

Thoughts of the Temperance Hall bring to mind a very popular concert party who made their debut there and afterwards gave shows all over the rural areas of the north. This party came into being when our only picture house was destroyed by fire and was out of commission for over six months. They were named the Kit Kaye Concert Party and were made up of local talent.

Many will remember the camp-fire scenes — "D.R.", James and his wife, Jock, Willy, Sandy, Clara, Jessie — swaying in rhythm to camp-fire songs. In harmony to gramophone records of music of South Sea islands and heads and necks with garlands of flowers!

The keenness of these amateurs made up for their lack of polished professionalism! "D.R.s" never-to-be-forgotten rendering of "The Auld Hoose" brought a nostalgic tear to many an eye. He was an exceptionally fine singer and would have done credit to any show.

Boxing? Yes, we had full houses at the boxing sessions. These were run on alternate Saturday nights in Wick and Thurso by the Woods Brothers, Dundee.

Names which come to mind — Bobbie Dobbs, Jim McCourt, Walter Lemmon, Fred Tennant, Eddie Beattie and I must not forget the locals who took part in a novice competition — "Tapsur", Battling Dodge, Tiger MacLeod, "Pym" Miller, "Rab", Harry "D" (from Wick).

These local lads, although inexperienced, put up a very good show and had enthusiastic support.

Many changes at Foyers

AT the halfway mark of the Great Glen, at a point on its Eastern side where the old road from Inverness to Fort Augustus leaves the shores of Loch Ness lies the two-tier village of Foyers.

Like most communities throughout the Highlands, Foyers was an early Pictish settlement and its name is derived from the 'old Gaelic' or 'Irish' word 'foither' meaning low lying land.

This name no doubt referred to the part of the village known as Lower Foyers which lies on the alluvial plain at the mouth of the river of the same name.

In an area surrounded by rocky crags and desolate uplands it is not surprising that settlement took place on the fertile soil around the river's mouth.

For centuries Foyers was primarily an agricultural community and during the 19th Century maintained a link with Inverness by water rather than by road.

There are still a number of people living in the village who remember when the Loch Ness steamer called at the old pier to pick up livestock and drop supplies.

Indeed many survive who as lads made a few extra pennies by driving the ponies and donkeys carrying supplies from the lochside up the steeply winding road to Upper Foyers.

In 1895 however, Foyers underwent its own industrial revolution when the British Aluminium Company decided to open a factory there.

What attracted the company was the cascading River Foyers, already made famous by its 90 foot waterfall, in which they saw the potential of a valuable energy source.

It was this billowing spume which gave the falls their Gaelic name "Eas na Smuid," meaning the smoking cataract!

12

Every summer thousands of visitors visit the falls retracing the step of such notable observers as the 18th Century lexographers Dr Samuel Johnston, his biographer Boswell and Robert Burns.

Burns in particular was very impressed by the spectacle and penned this small poem on the spot:

> Among the heathy hills and rugged woods,
> The roaring Foyers pours his mossy floods,
> Till full he dashes on the rocky mounds,
> Where through a shapeless breach his stream resounds,
> As high in the air the bursting torrents flow,
> As deep recoiling surges foam below,
> Prone down, and rock the whitening sheet descends,
> And viewless, echo's ear astonished rends,
> Dim seen through rising mist and ceaseless showers,
> The hoary cavern wide resounding lowers,
> Still through the gap the struggling river toils,
> And still below the horrid cauldron boils.

For many years most of the land around the village was the property of the Frasers of Foyers whose home was a mansion house, no longer existing, close to the site of the Aluminium factory.

Today the most noted building in the vicinity is Boleskine House some two miles to the east.

Boleskine was built by Archibald Fraser in 1800 on the site of the old Boleskine Church whose parish included the village of Foyers.

At the turn of this century the fortunes of the old house took a rather sinister turn when it was bought by Aleister Crowley at that time known as 'the most evil man in the world.'

In common with many artists and public figures of the time Crowley had an obsessive passion for the black arts and is today remembered as the most accomplished occultist of his time by believers in the supernatural.

It was at Boleskine that he perfected the magical ceremony of Abra Melin working in a room of the house which he converted into his chapel.

Today Boleskine House still hits the headlines from time to time having recently become the property of millionaire pop artist Jimmy Page of Led Zeppelin.

For seven years Hugh Fraser, of Foyers, took refuge in the hills after Culloden and although, the Redcoats hunted him day and night, his cave of concealment was never divulged. The local people nicknamed him Bonaid Odhair — Dun-bonnet — and could openly talk of him, while the soldiers never discovered his true identity.

The cave appears to have been well hidden in a district known as the Camus, and near it is a yew tree, from which the Frasers took wood for their bows and arrows in earlier days. One story tells of a girl bringing food to the fugitive, being followed by a soldier guessing her errand. But the old laird spotted the man long before he reached the retreat, shot him dead in his tracks, and later buried him where he fell.

Another day a boy, carrying a cask of beer, was met by a party of Government soldiers on a brae near the falls of Foyers, and questioned on the whereabouts of his master. But the stout lad refused to divulge the secret, even though the soldiers slashed off one of his hands. The cask tumbled off the lad's shoulders and into the chasm below, since known as the Cask's Leap.

Ardersier . . .
where ghosts lurk

A HUNDRED years ago if you travelled east from Inverness along the southern coast of the Moray Firth it would not have been long before the tall masts of the Ardersier fishing fleet came into sight.

For although today hardly a rowing boat is to be seen on the beach of this windswept coastal village there was a time when almost every able-bodied man there made his living from the one time rich offshore fishing.

Evidence of Ardersier's sea-going heritage remains in the fact that it is one of the few Highland villages where fishermen's thatched cottages remain, alas, today untended and probably soon destined to disappear. The proof that fishing in the village was a hazardous business, claiming the lives of many men, lies in the village burial ground where a large number of tombstones mark the last resting places of the drowned.

In those days long line fishing was the main industry of Ardersier before pollution and mechanised netting put an end to the shoals of whitefish which fed in the firth.

In the centre of the village is the Ship Inn which still retains the atmosphere of a fisherman's pub and even now some of the older men who spent their youth on the boats still frequent the 200 year old hostelry. The Ship was thatched until around 1912 when the roofing was replaced by slate and in more recent years the exterior of the building was modernised.

Adjacent to the inn is a three-storey store where local farmers used to load their grain on to ships which in those days could dock immediately alongside in a channel cut inshore.

Nothing remains of the Ardersier Pier except a few stumps jutting from the wet sand.

Perhaps this is not such a sad loss as while it stood it was generally shunned by the village fishermen who resented paying pier dues to tie up there.

On the Inverness side of Ardersier lies the farm of Lonnie whose property includes a low bridge hardly visible now.

An old story tells of a local practical joker who laid in wait for a ploughboy who had gone to Newton of Petty on a dark winter's night to have his plough irons sharpened.

The joker covered himself in a sheet when the lad was passing and leapt out on him, pretending to be a ghost.

The unfortunate ending to the story is that the ploughboy swung the heavy irons from his shoulder and brought them down full force on the 'ghost's' head leaving him lifeless on the bridge. The village of Ardersier for many years has been split between two great Highland estates, that of the Earl of Cawdor and that of the Earl of Moray.

Nearby Castle Stuart in the old days was the property of the Earl of Moray, and although never a family seat served as the local centre of administration.

Castle Stuart was built in the early part of the 17th Century by Earl James Moray, son of the Bonnie Earl.

The castle for many years has been surrounded by tales of ghosts and many local people still believe it to be haunted. A local story tells of four lads who decided to spend the night in a haunted room of the Castle.

In the morning all four emerged muted and unwilling to tell of what had passed there, and as a result one of them went insane.

A drover encamped near the castle also declared that he would spend the night in the haunted room but was found the next morning lying on the stone paving beneath the window.

One of the most notable Churches in the Highlands lies also in the Ardersier area — the old Kirk of Petty (West). It is here that the remains of the famous MacGillivray of Dumnaglass were buried after his heroic and fatal stand at the Battle of Culloden, where he killed no less than 15 redcoats before he was cut down.

It is believed that his body was originally buried in a trench with many of his followers by Cumberland's men, who stood guard over it for six weeks forbidding the removal of the remains.

But after that period they departed and the trench was opened, the stench killed with whisky and MacGillivray's remains removed to Petty.

Giant Power Heidelberg Electric Belt

Sent on 10 Days' Free Trial

Victorians firmly believed in the magic curative properties of electricity. The Heidelberg electric belt guaranteed "the relief and cure of all chronic and nervous diseases, disorders and weaknesses peculiar to men." It was not cheap: £4.50. That was a great deal of money, then.

Mr John Mackenzie received this memento in 1881 for putting out posters for the first two issues of the Northern Chronicle. Originally he was due for 10s (50p) but at the last minute the manager decided 7s 6d (35½p) would suffice!

VIN VITAE

Wine of Life

A NEW AND PERFECT TONIC STIMULANT FOR THE TIRED, WEAK AND SICK OF ALL CLASSES. A RENEWER OF ENERGY, A STIMULANT FOR THE FATIGUED, A STRENGTHENER FOR THE WEAK, AN EFFECTIVE AND AGREEABLE FOOD FOR THE BLOOD, BRAIN AND NERVES.

Vin Vitae gives health and strength.

YOU SHOULD TAKE

VIN VITAE

REGULARLY IF YOU MUST ANSWER

YES

TO ANY ONE OF THESE QUESTIONS.

Are you Easily Tired?
Do you Sleep Badly?
Are you Nervous?
Do you Feel Exhausted?
Have you Lost your Appetite?
Is your Stomach Weak?
Are you Thin?
Is your Circulation Poor?
Are you Weak, either constitutionally or from recent sickness?

"Vin Vitae" was described as "a preparation combining, through the highest medical skill, the curative powers of vegetable elements procured from South American herbs and the tonic effects of Californian wines." Cost: 25p per bottle.

B

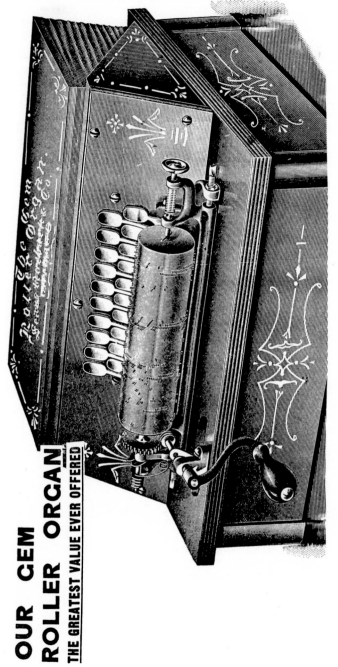

OUR GEM
ROLLER ORGAN
THE GREATEST VALUE EVER OFFERED

This beautifully made little organ, selling in the '80s at around £1, was deservedly a favourite musical instrument in thousands of homes. An immense range of roll music was available at 50p a dozen.

Prominent in the life of Ardersier is the nearby stronghold of Fort George completed in 1767 and which until recently housed successive regiments whose men brought a new lease of life to the village. The site of Fort George was originally intended to be on the Longman in Inverness but the Town Council objected to this plan and it was decided that the present location was just as ideal.

Traces of an earlier fort however, remain at Cromal Mount near Ardersier (the name being a contraction of Cromwell).

It is interesting to note that the original village of Ardersier lay to the east of Fort George but today little remains of this on the shiftless sands.

The new village grew up in its present location no doubt due to the traffic between Fort George and Inverness. There is some conjectures as to the derivation of the word Ardersier, some claiming that it comes from the Gaelic Ard-na-saor meaning the Cape of the Carpenters and others that it was originally Ard-ros-iar (the Point to the West).

Although today the traditional industries of Ardersier have completely vanished modern commerce has brought the village a new lease of life in the form of a thriving new industrial estate close by.

When TV was
but a shadow

I WONDER how many people had the privilege of viewing TV in Thurso as far back as 1933-34? I remember the late Peter Peraccini, radio engineer, was experimenting with the intricacies of TV reception. Television was then broadcast from Alexandra Palace on the Baird system and Peter had a real "Heath Robinson" contraption rigged up in his workshop (now occupied by W. Brass). As far as I can remember, the picture was received on a small rectangular valve or tube about 2 by 1½ inches, surrounded by wires and valves. There was a large disc in front and this had holes on the outer edge. The disc was rotated at a certain speed and the picture (such as it was) was viewed through these holes. One must remember this was in the very elementary stages of TV and when one saw a shadow or slight movement, this was interpreted as a picture. Peter must have had loads of patience and spent many hours experimenting. I was talking to him just after the 1939-45 war and he told me that in all the years of work in his profession this episode gave him his greatest thrill.

There was a drapery in the lower end of the town and the owner took a delight in playing tricks on the young lads. One trick he used to play was to tie one end of a long piece of cotton thread to a half-crown and leave it on the pavement just outside his door — in his view! The unsuspecting finder would bend to pick up the coin, and he, who had the other end of the thread, would jerk the coin into the shop. Another victim! One victim "got his own back". The draper had already tricked this lad. So, armed with a pair of scissors, the lad crept on his hands and knees past the window — snip — grabbed the coin and disappeared as quick as lightning with his prize, which, I think, for his enterprise, he thoroughly deserved.

Now and again we were able to earn an honest penny. During furniture sales we'd borrow a two-wheeled "cartie" from a shop-keeper and canvass the buyers at the sale for any "chobbies". Usually we would get a few coppers for transporting a chair or table to the buyer's home and sometimes we'd have a load and only get a word of thanks! I assure you, we'd steer clear of that customer next time!

"A penny line" — "halfpenny worth of hooks and a twopenny canie!" What a trade in these articles the ironmongers must have had. Then, down to the harbour or breakwater to fish for "sellags" or "peltags". We spent many hours of enjoyment around that area, and never seemed to feel the cold dressed only in a "ganzie" (jersey), short trousers and bare feet in sand-shoes. Perhaps we'd go a short distance "up 'e river" and catch the conger-eels, then, should there be a schooner in the harbour, try and sell them to the Swedish or Norwegian crews for a few coppers. We'd then go up to "Choes" or Mrs Norn's sweet-shops to spend our earnings. I saw a photo recently in an old copy of "The John O'Groat Journal" (Christmas Number, dated December 1927). There was a view of Thurso harbour and in the foreground were about a dozen young boys fishing. They were lying on their tummies, some barefooted, and one lad had his shirt-tail sticking out of a hole in his trousers. How typical of the lads who used to frequent the harbour, who had to put on their oldest clothes before going fishing — well, they set out with that intention but one couldn't guess what devilment they'd be up to before the night was over!

The stories
of Culloden

THE most popular excursion within easy distance of Inverness, among the tourists who come to the Highlands, is undoubtedly to Culloden Moor and the scene of the famous battle. There are countless stories and legends deriving from the battle and its sequel. Some are factual and documented; others are less reliable — though none the less fascinating for that!

Culloden Home Farm and Culloden House certainly had close ties with the events of the '45 Rebellion. The site of the House was Culloden Castle, historically important as having sheltered both Prince Charlie and the Duke of Cumberland within a few days. The Prince slept there (one of his few authentic resting places) the night before the battle. Then the Duke moved in, but made a longer visit!

In the dungeons, the only existing parts of the former castle, below the house, seventeen officers of the Jacobite army were confined for three days, then taken outside and shot. Another story says they were hanged from an old tree in front of the house. No matter what may have been their end, they were undoubtedly murdered in cold blood by the order of "Butcher Cumberland."

Near the entrance to Culloden House, incidentally, an old tree stump used to carry a set of "branks" or Scold's Bridle, to which offenders were fixed, so that they could neither sit down nor stand erect. It was often used to "check the tongues of over-garrulous women."

At Resaurie they still tell of a local man who made a heroic and historical stand at Culloden during which he killed 13 Redcoats wielding only a timber wrenched from a farm cart. As the enemy approached they couldn't get near him, and only managed to succeed in overpowering him by climbing over the roof of the barn. As he struggled for his life, an officer of the English army shouted to his men to spare him and take him prisoner, as surely he was a brave man; but the soldiers appeared not to hear him, and he was slain where he stood.

Near Gask Mains there is the legend of John MacGillivray, known as "Big John of the Markets," who was reported killed at Culloden after having slain 14 men with his broadsword. Far from having lost his life, so the story goes, he escaped to America where he became a Colonel in a Royalist regiment in the War of Independence!

By the roadside are Stone Circles, vestiges of Druid times, standing on a slight hillock on the farm land of Gask. It was here that the Clan MacGillivray representatives at Culloden halted on the way to the battle, and sharpened their broadswords and dirks on the largest of the stones. Marks on the surface, still to be seen, are said to have been made by those swords.

Another MacGillivray story runs as follows: At the time of Culloden a young herd boy from Riereach, attracted by the sound of gunfire, climbed to the top of Tor-buiach, a small promontory not far from Easter Galcantray, and watched the battle in progress. He then ran back for a meal, and later in the evening was so curious that he went down to the battlefield to get a closer look. Spotted by some English soldiers, he was captured and questioned and detained until the following Monday engaged in digging graves. His payment was a MacGillivray tartan kilt, which he took back to his employer; and it is believed that the kilt or part of it is still in existence.

A mile or so beyond Achlean stands Roderick MacKenzie's cairn marking the spot where one of Scotland's little-known heroes fell dying for the cause of his Prince.

Prince Charlie was in hiding in the district after Culloden, and although he is known to have spent a little while with the Seven Men of Glenmoriston in their cave at Corrie Doe, he must have found refuge in other similar caves in these bleak heather-clad hills.

Roderick MacKenzie was a loyal and trusted officer in the Jacobite army, and constantly by the side of the Prince, who on this occasion was in danger of being captured at any moment since the King's soldiers were gradually surrounding the cave in which they were concealed. Roderick quickly realised that something had to be done, and, as he bore a distinct resemblance to the Prince, decided on a plan.

21

And so, while sleeping in the cave, he was aroused by voices in the glen, and, going to the mouth of the cave, he could see figures of approaching Redcoats. Without a word he crept towards the sleeping Prince and quietly took his plaid and bonnet; then, having put them on, stole outside and down the glen.

When within firing distance of the Redcoats, he broke into the open and started to run. At once the soldiers spotted him and followed in pursuit, firing at him as they went; and as a bullet hit him he fell to the ground shouting:

"You've killed your Prince! You've killed your Prince."

Thinking him to be the Young Pretender, the soldiers immediaely cut off his head and carried it in triumph to Fort Augustus, where they presented it to the Duke of Cumberland after Jacobite prisoners had identified it as the head of Prince Charlie. The Duke set off in haste for London, but it was soon discovered that a mistake had been made, as the Prince was found to be still at large!

A less heroic story is told of a man by the name of Corrie who lived at Fort Augustus. Having heard of the battle and the subsequent atrocities, he decided to make it his task to rid the country of the Duke. So he took up a position near Glendoebeag where he hoped to ambush the Duke. But when the troopers arrived his nerve failed him and he ran along Glendoe Burn to hide in a cave on Loch Ness side. To this day it is known as Corrie's Cave.

Another story tells of a Highland piper retreating from Culloden approached Torgoyle Inn when he heard horse's hooves galloping behind him; and, hiding behind a boulder, he slashed out with his sword when a redcoated figure flashed by. The blow severed the soldier's head, and the piper swooped on the body to retrieve any spoil. The boots of the rider were the greatest temptation, but, try as he might, they would not come off. However, not to be outdone, he took legs and all, and continued on his way to the inn. Alas! no accommodation was available, and he had to find lodgings in the byre, beside the inn-keeper's cow.

Early next morning, when the dairymaid went out to milk the cow, she saw the boots lying in the stall, and, unaware that the piper was also sleeping in the byre, she ran back to the inn with the frightful tale that the cow had eaten the traveller, and only his legs were spared! However, before the true facts were known, the cow was shot and buried!

Culloden stories! Truly, tales without end!

Murder of the Provost

BORLUM farm, south of Inverness, has a tale worth telling.

About five hundred years ago it fell in to the hands of a family of MacKintoshes, remained so until the early 18th century, and being a sept of the Clan Chattan, living in an outpost of the Mac-Kintosh country, they were compelled to be on the lookout for invading armies, and assist in their final expulsion if they should invade. As a consequence of holding such a precarious position, they became formidable and ferocious, the scourge of the district. Indeed, they were a wild lot, dangerous even to their friends.

Two of the fiercest representatives of that family, Lord and Lady Borlum, lived in the time of James V, and the story of the murder of the venerable Provost Junor of Inverness is told in *Historical and Traditional Sketches of Highland Families and the Highlands*, by an Inverness centenarian of the last century, John MacLean. He relates:

"The Laird's lady on one occasion went to Inverness, where her visits would be most agreeably dispensed with; or, in other words, her absence would be considered good company by the terrified inhabitants. She was followed by two mischievous imps, as train bearers, or lady's henchmen. In the course of her perambulations through the town, she was seen by the worthy Provost in a position 'that mantled to his cheek the blush of shame,' and he was so shocked at her rude and indelicate demeanour that he took courage to reprove her, exclaiming: 'O, fie, fie, Lady Borlum'."

She was furious. The author vividly describes how, raising herself to her full height, she slowly turned away her flaming eye, saying, "You shall pay dearly for this," and passed on.

Home she went to tell her husband, and together they planned revenge. Their two sons were assigned the deed, and when the Provost made his usual evening stroll towards Campfield (now

23

believed to be on the Essich road near the town boundaries) the sons set upon him, stabbed him to death, then hid his body under a bush, where it was later found.

Strong suspicions at once rested on the Borlum family, and after a day or two there seemed no doubt about the assassins, and as John MacLean writes:

"Meetings after meetings were held to bring them to punishment; but the town council, although eager enough to avenge the death of their chief magistrate, dreaded the ferocity and power of Borlum (who was a member of the council), the more particularly as he was backed by the friendship and power of the Earl of Huntly, at that time exercising almost regal authority in the north, and by whom black MacKintosh of Borlum was always protected from the consequences of his evil deeds. The council, therefore, however reluctantly, were obliged to abandon the idea of punishing the assassins, and all they could do to show their respect for the deceased provost, and their detestation and horror of his murders, was to pass a resolution that no member of the Borlum family should ever be eligible for a seat in the town council of Inverness — a resolution ever after adhered to."

Black cats
are evil!

AS YOU journey from the mainland to the Isle of Lewis, maybe on a sunny day on holiday, in modern comfort and safety, keep a sharp look out for cats. Yes, cats! For cats are indeed associated with such a journey — one that ended in disaster.

It happened long, long ago and the central character of the story was John Garve Macgillichallum, of Razay. John's exploits had made him a considerable heroic celebrity not least because he invariably put his courage and talents to the best uses. Most of all he was renowned for his implacable antagonism to the sisterhood of witches, many of whom he had despatched in the course of his adventures. Not surprisingly, the witches of the Highlands had sworn to exact their revenge but, cunning and patient, they bided their time . . .

It so happened that John and his companions were planning an expedition to Lewis to hunt deer. In due course all preparations were made and he and his young friends embarked in the chieftain's yacht and it was not long before they were engaged in a most successful hunt in the mountains. That night they returned to their shooting quarters where they spent some happy hours in song and drinking before retiring.

Next morning they prepared for the return journey to Razay. It was squally and boisterous and the seas were running high. Nevertheless, John was not deterred by the elements and was all for setting sail. His friends were more cautious, however, and urged him to put off the journey until conditions were less hazardous. John was adamant, but he did suggest that before they went aboard they might adjourn to the ferry house for a few drams. Understandably there was little objection to this, and off they went. While they were thus agreeably employed, an old hag hobbled into the ferry house on a crutch. The argument about sailing, now fortified by

25

a succession of drams, was waxing strong but getting nowhere. Casting about for support, John suddenly saw the old woman and asked for her opinion. Without hesitation she agreed with him that the party should set sail at once. You never know, she said, conditions might get worse the longer you wait. It was enough. John issued the order and all embarked.

The moment they were under sail he regretted his decision, for the ferocity of the wind increased and the seas became mountainous. But try as they would they could not put back to Lewis so he made the best of a bad job and strove might and main to keep his sights on the lofty point of Aird in Skye. His companions rallied around him and hope began to mount that all would, in the end, be well.

Sudddenly, to the amazement of all beholders, a huge cat was seen to be climbing the rigging. Then another appeared and it, too, swarmed up the ropes. Then another, and another and another . . . until shrouds, masts and the whole tackle were covered with huge cats. Only one man of the entire ship's company was not dumb-founded. That was John. He knew well enough what the cats were. Turning to his companions and shouting to make himself heard above the storm, he called:

"These are not cats you see before you, but witches. Kill them before they kill us!"

So saying, he drew his sword and advanced upon the cats determined to sell his life dearly. But it was not to be. At the command of the largest and most ferocious cat clinging to the very top of the mast, all made a concerted movement and overturned the vessel. In an instant it was swallowed up by the waves and everyone aboard perished.

As John and his doomed party were struggling hopelessly in the wild waters amid the gleeful howling of the triumphant witches, another hero of the endless battle against the sisterhood of Satan was seated comfortably before a roaring fire in his hunting hut at Badenoch. Beside him lay his faithful hounds, his gun and his knife. Outside raged a wild storm.

Hunter of the Hills, as he was known, reflected that there were worse places to be on such a night than in a snug hut before a blazing fire of aromatic logs. Musing thus, he was surprised to hear the wailing of a cat at the door. He was immediately suspicious for, with John of Razay, he was renowned for his pursuit and punishment of witches in the Highlands and was well aware that they most commonly took the form of cats. Nevertheless he opened the door and beheld a bedraggled, shivering cat cowering in the rain. At once the cat pleaded with him.

"Great Hunter of the Hills," it said, "I know your hatred of my craft and, possibly, it is well justified. But spare me, I beg you. I come to you for protection from the cruelty and oppression of my sisterhood."

Moved, somewhat, by the creature's pleading, the Hunter pacified his snarling dogs and invited the cat in. But the creature hesitated.

"I am grateful for your kindness," it said, "but I fear you will not be able to control your dogs. Would you please be so kind as to bind them with this long hair so that I may feel secure?"

The Hunter narrowed his eyes. There was something peculiar about that long hair. So he pretended to agree, but instead of binding the dogs by their necks as the cat had asked he wound it around a beam of wood. Deceived, the cat then advanced to the fire and sat down as if to dry itself. In a matter of seconds it began to grow. The Hunter jokingly asked if all was well, and the cat replied that it was just the fur expanding because of the warmth. But worse was to come. The cat grew to an enormous size and then in an instant transformed itself into the likeness of the Goodwife of Laggan.

"Hunter," she said with a cackle, "your hour has come. You see before you the avowed champion of my devoted sisterhood of whom you and Macgillichallum of Razay were always the most relentless of enemies. But I can tell you that Razay is no more. He today lies dead at the bottom of the sea . . . and now comes your turn to die."

So saying, and assuming a terrifying appearance, she made a spring for the Hunter. But instantly the two dogs, which she had believed to be securely fastened, leapt at her in turn and a most ferocious conflict ensued. Alarmed by this unexpected turn of events, the witch, frenziedly exclaimed: "Fasten, hair; fasten." But all the hair could do was to tighten around the log. The dogs had their teeth firmly sunk in the witch and she raced off trying to shake them loose. But not until she had magically drawn every tooth in their heads was she free. Then she turned herself into a raven and fled over the mountains in the direction of her home.

The unfortunate dogs perished almost at once and after burying them the Hunter returned home to his family. His wife was not there when he arrived but made her appearance soon after saying that she had been to see the Goodwife of Laggan who was desperately ill of a sudden fever. The Hunter heard this news with no surprise and resolved to visit the Goodwife himself. On arrival he found all the neighbours around the cottage in a very melancholy group believing that a good and virtuous friend was nearing her death.

The Hunter pushed past them and, walking up to the Goodwife's bed, stripped it of the coverings. As the neighbours looked on in amazement he declared: "Look at the object of all your solitude! She is nothing more than a self-confessed witch. Today she told me that she and her infernal companions had consigned the Laird of Razay to his death at sea and she then attempted to seal my doom too. This night, however, it will be she that will lose her life."

He then recounted all the happenings in the forest hut and pointed out the wounds which his hounds had inflicted upon her. The witch thereupon confessed and pleaded for forgiveness, but before anyone could say another word she expired.

At just about this time another neighbour who was returning home from Strathdearn was entering the forest of Monalea, in Badenoch, when he was surprised to see a woman in black running at top speed. She paused for a moment to ask if he thought she could reach the churchyard of Dalarossie by midnight. He replied that she might if she kept up the same breathless pace. The woman then fled along the road uttering loud lamentations. A few miles further on the traveller met a large black dog bounding along the road as if in pursuit of the woman. Then came a big black man on a big black horse galloping at top speed in the same direction. The rider slowed down and called: "Have you seen a woman followed by a dog?" "Yes," said the traveller. "Do you think the dog will overtake her before she can reach the church at Dalarossie?" The traveller said it would be a close thing.

He then continued on his way marvelling at what he had experienced. But he had proceeded only a mile or two when the rider overtook him on his return. The woman's body was lying across the bow of the saddle, and the dog was still hanging on to her with its teeth. They disappeared into the night.

When he reached home the traveller recounted his remarkable tale but was soon made aware of the company he had met on the road. All agreed that it must have been the spirit of the Wife of

Laggan flying for protection from the infernal spirits to the church-yard of Dalarossie — which was well known to be so sacred a place that a witch making her pilgrimage to it would at once be purified. But it seemed that the Goodwife of Laggan was not quite fleet enough of foot . . .

◆◆◆

Here are a few of the many sayings, recipes and cures which emanate from Rosemarkie:

When the robins come back to the gardens too early it is the sign of a bad winter to come. Equally indicative of a bad winter is a heavy blossom on the broom.

He who waits long at the ferry will get across sometime.

A light-heeled mother makes a leaden-heeled daughter.

May ye ne'er want a friend nor a dram to gie him.

If Candlemas be clear and fair, the half of the winter is to go and mair. If Candlemas be dark and full, the half of winter is past at Yule.

A dewy May and a rainy June; the farmer up and the gardener doon.

Cure for diarrheoa: slows made into jam.

Cure for a sore throat: the sole of a sweaty sock tied around the throat at night.

Prayer for the hungry: O Lord when hunger pinches sore, do thou stand us in stead and send us from thy bounteous store a tup or wether head. Amen.

In the days when the herring trade was at its height in Caithness, large quantities were landed at Scrabster. Many of them were sold from small "kerties" drawn by horses with the vendor walking alongside calling "Herreen, fresh herreen" and reinforcing his shouts with an old motor horn. In those days herring cost 9d to 1s a dozen — but they were cheaper still to the youngsters who used to get the cheery invitation from the fishermen: "Help yourself."

(The same happy generosity exists today. Early in 1975 at Ullapool with my daughter from California, fishermen on the quay-side filled a plastic bag with herring for us for no more payment than a big smile! When we got home to Inverness we counted over three dozen! — Nancy Reid).

Where every corner whispers history

EAST of Inverness, twelve miles as the soldier marches and nine as the gull flies, on a stoney promontory opposite Chanonry Point, lies Fort George. Within the red sandstone — quarried at Muir of Ord — ramparts, a wealth of history, tradition and military lore whispers from every corner of the irregular polygon.

On a recent visit I observed with satisfaction and pleasure the fine, painstaking work of restoration currently being carried out by the Office of Works. Which brings one to the guns.

On the shore beside the old harbour — The "Crab's Pond" of boyhood days — rested, freshly painted, two mortars and mountings, presumably awaiting removal to sites in the bastions.

Originally, the six bastions were armed with 18-twenty-four pounders; 25-eighteen-pounders; 22-twelve-pounders; and four, 13-inch mortars. The story goes that the first governor appointed to command Fort George was being conducted round by the resident architect. On the north-east bastion the architect, with a sweep of his arms, proudly proclaimed "There, General, we have built for you an impregnable fortress."

The old warrior raised his cane and pointed towards Cromal Hill, a mile to the east.

"What about an enemy planting a few mortars yonder?", he enquired.

It is said the mortified architect shot himself the same evening in the yard of the grand magazine!

By the '60's, the armament had been reduced to four twelve-pounders; eight eighteen-pounders; six 68-pounders; three ten-inch smooth-bore guns; and two 13-inch mortars.

In the early '90's the guns were removed to Woolwich Arsenal by sea, with the loss of one soldier drowned. A gun barrel slipped from the sling as it was being hoisted on board the W.D. vessel, crashed through the loading barge alongside carrying with it one of the fatigue party. For his gallantry in repeatedly diving to free his comrade, Charles Ratcliffe was awarded the Humane Society Medal.

At Aldershot in '05 this fine soldier, on discharge to pension, gave me his spotlessly white canvas fatigue suit.

As a final salute to the old cannon, my parents occupied the "Master Gunner's Quarters" and the name recalls a happy childhood in far away Victorian days.

◆◆◆

Craigmonie, the rocky hill to the rear of Lewiston and Drumnadrochit, was the scene of the last stand made by the Vikings in the early centuries, and the hill is still crowned with the remains of ancient fortifications. Tradition relates that Monie, son of the King of Scandinavia, landed in Argyll with a large force accompanied by his sister.

His retreat to the ships was cut off and he was chased northwards until he took refuge in Craigmonie. After fierce fighting, however, the Norsemen were driven to the plain below and slaughttered. Happily, Monie's sister escaped this fate. She took refuge in a cave where she was discovered by the Highlanders when searching for their dead. They showed her mercy and she made her life with them in the region. The cave in which she hid is sometimes known in the locality as the "Bed of the King's daughter" and sometimes as "Queen Mary's Rock." There is no evidence, however, that the Scots Queen was ever in this vicinity.

It was old-clothes
night for the police

MUNICIPAL Election Results night.   Now! they were nights to remember.   University Student election rags had nothing on this!

The elections in these days were held around October, and how the dark nights suited the purpose.   Even the police had to don their oldest uniforms when on duty at the square in the evening.   I have seen the square filled to capacity and the population of Thurso was only between 3,000 and 4,000 then!   The people started to assemble around 7 p.m. and by 9 p.m., the fun (if you could call it that) was at its height.

Missiles were many and varied.   Fireworks, rotten fruit, eggs, ochre, flour, even potatoes.   In fact, next morning, one wondered if anything of a throwable nature was left.   Policemen were the recipients of a great many missiles — being in front of the crowd and who could resist a policeman's hat, especially if the culprit had the perfect opportunity of getting away with it?   How easy it was to aim, throw and dodge to another part of the crowded area.

Strange though it may seem I have never heard of anybody being arrested on "Election Night".   When the Town Hall door was opened to allow some dignitary to enter or leave this was the signal for a broadside of missiles.   (How about it Town Improvements Committee?   Here is a suggestion which would go with a bang!   I am sure you would be able to persuade some volunteers — a battle between the "up 'e tooners" and "doon 'e tooners".   What a finale for Gala Week!   I would suggest the beach for this battle — tide times studied beforehand, of course!)

The Returning Officer should have received a medal for his bravery — having to appear on the steps of the Town Hall doorway to announce the results.   It would now be about 11 p.m. but there was always a big reserve of ammunition kept for this part of the

OUR PARLOR SPECIAL

THIS CLOCK CASE IS MADE OF WOOD, covered with a secret preparation in imitation of black marble. This clock, wiped with a damp cloth at intervals, will always keep as new. It is guaranteed not to chip, warp or wear off and always retains its appearance of genuine black Italian marble.

THE CLOCK IS ORNAMENTED with four handsome gold plated scrolls. It stands upon beautiful metal feet made to match the balance of the scroll work. The dial of the clock is one of the very latest productions, being fancy rococo embossed pattern. The numerals are Arabic ones. Height of clock is 12½ inches; width of clock, 9¾ inches; depth of clock, 4½ inches.

No. 5R7615

There are possibly still a number of these ornate "Parlour Specials" in use — for Victorians made things to last! This decorative clock would have cost you about £1.50 at the turn of the century.

*Although the Great War was not over (as was confidently predicted) by
December, 1914, consolation was readily to hand at 15p a bottle! That,
however, was equivalent to about £5 today . . .*

STUDEBAKER FOUR £245

ELECTRIC SELF-STARTER AND DYNAMO LIGHTING SET.

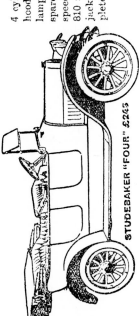

STUDEBAKER "FOUR" £245

4 cyl. eginne, touring body, hcod, screen, 6 electric lamps, detachable rims, spare rim and tyre carrier, speedometer, electric horn, 810 × 90 Continental tyres, jack, pump, tools, complete ready for the road—

£245.

The Studebaker "Four" gives every promise of being the Car of the Season, just as its predecessor, the 15-20 h.p. was unquestionably the Car of 1913. Write for complete specification.

IMMEDIATE DELIVERY.   *TRIAL RUN BY APPOINTMENT.*

Agents for INVERNESS-SHIRE, ROSS-SHIRE, and SUTHERLANDSHIRE—

ROBERTSON & PORTER, ENGINEERS,

DINGWALL & STRATHPEFFER.

If one of those 1914 Studebaker tourers were available in good condition today, collectors would give thousands for it. But even at £245, it was far beyond the reach of the ordinary family 60 years ago.

C

WHAT SIXPENCE WILL DO.

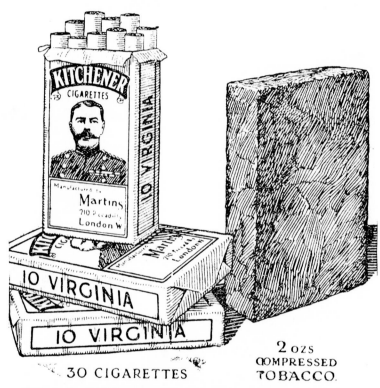

30 CIGARETTES

2 OZS
COMPRESSED
TOBACCO.

Early in the 1914-18 war, many organisations led the way in providing comforts for the troops — and the Northern Chronicle was no exception. Every 2½p sent in by a reader enabled it to send off to a fighting man three packets of "Kitchener" cigarettes and 2 oz. of tobacco, together with the name and address of the donor.

proceedings and also to "pelt" the newly appointed councillors and their supporters. And, unluckily for them, as there was only one exit from the Town Hall they had to run the gauntlet. Everybody seemed to take it all in good part and you counted yourself unlucky should you be on the receiving end of a rotten egg!

You can imagine the mess which had to be cleaned up the following morning! Mr Langley, the burgh surveyor at that time, soon had his stalwarts on the job, and as his team were the local Fire Brigade they brought their equipment and hosed the area down. I was employed in one of the shops in the area for a time and I had my share of cleaning rotten eggs, fruit, etc., off the windows and doorways of our premises. I didn't grumble; after all, I had helped in making the mess!

Parliamentary candidates had their share of missiles and heckling. It seemed "Sir Erchie" was our darling, and to us, anybody who should dare oppose him, was in for a tough time! After all, he was "weel kent" in the streets of Thurso and always had a cheery smile and wave for us. Also he financed a "bun-fecht" (tea-party) in the Salvation Army Hall for us during Christmas. That was all the interest we had in politics anyway! I have been told by one of our elder citizens that at one eve-of-poll meeting, some enterprising (?) youths released a basket of pigeons in the crowded hall. When the results were announced — and invariably "Sir Erchie" was "in" again — there was a trek to Thurso Castle to take part in the celebrations.

Days of music and laughter

PERHAPS it's the nostalgia for lost youth which always surrounds my childhood days in Innes Street, Inverness, with an aura of sunshine, music and laughter. Certainly the sheer joy of roller-skating or running barefoot up and down the flat, even concrete pavement was a thrilling experience on a hot summer's day . . . and were those hot summer days as numerous as my memory suggests?

It's a pity someone did not gather all the Inverness children's street-play, songs and rhymes of the thirties, as they appear to be that little bit different from other parts of Scotland. For instance, I had never heard of "Peevers" (Hop Scotch) until I grew up and realised that they were a form of our "Beddies" which we played with "Skeetchies" made from bits of glazed tiles which we found outside the fireplace store near the Rose Street Foundry. While we searched for "Skeetchies" there, the boys gathered the round metallic shilling-like off-cuts from the machines and chinked them in their pockets to make believe they had money to jingle.

Invernessians are well-known for adding "ee" or "ie" to the end of familiar words in a kind of endearing fashion, i.e. "The old wifie" or "Wee Mannie" — or "Bakie's Shoppie".

"Bakie's Shoppie" was our equivalent of the modern teenage cafe. Mine Host was Miss Rebecca, who served groceries to our parents and mouth-watering sweets and worldy-wise advice to us. It was the height of sophistication to sit on an upturned crate in "Bakies" sucking a "Sherbert Fountain" through a liquorice straw, watching the world go by!

There never seemed to be a dull moment in our street; and the residents themselves were a varied collection.

Most of them were long-suffering as far as children's noise was concerned but there were some who did not like children (often the childless ones). They made a point of keeping any ball which happened to fall into their pocket-handkerchief front gardens. However the boys meted out rough justice by waiting until it was dark, tying a string to the knocker or one of the large jangling bell-pulls and then keeping up regular door-knocking or bell-ringing until they wore out their victims.

At midday and in the evenings, the streets would be thronged with "black spots" moving three and four abreast down the street and making for over the Black Bridge. Those would be the men in dungarees going home from work at the Railway or Foundry Workshops. What cheery fellows they seemed to be in those days of hard work, long hours and low wages. They never passed us without a word of greeting or flicking a cigarette card of our favourite filmstars.

At Hallowe'en time, every door was open to us (except for the few meanies, like the ball-keeping ones and other odd-bods) but we had to work hard for our nuts and apples. None of us stood dumb on the doorstep or on the floor, waiting for our "Hallowe'en", without giving anything in return. We practised our "turns" and planned our disguises weeks beforehand.

We even gave our own "Concerts" in our back garden — which was hardly a garden, merely a back-green shared by other tenants in the building. My father rigged up a "Stage" (a large wooden platform) for us and many a budding trouper showed his/her paces there, to the accompaniment of cries of encouragement or derisive catcalls from the critical audience. I don't think money was idolised in the same way in those days because, although our "Concert" would be packed full, the entrance fee was nominal — more-or-less as a token. I remember paying two pins as an entrance fee to view a showing of a Laurel and Hardy film on a cinematograph owned by one of my brother's friends. At the time, it never occurred to me to wonder what he did with the thirty or so pins he received — unless his mother was a keen dressmaker, or practised acupuncture!

Sometimes we would have to stop our street games because of a procession of horses, each with a long, low wooden trailer on wheels (as long as a modern articulated lorry) on which there was balanced a huge tree-trunk like a telegraph pole. This procession went at a snail's pace and was headed for the sawmill on the shore. The boys used to enjoy the ride down the street by the side of the driver or at the back of the trailer.

One of the boys' favourites was "Charlie the Drover", who drove the sheep and cattle down the street to their doom in the slaughter-house, to be made into mince, sausages and "trolleybags" (the name we used for the sheeps' udders which were used for making haggis, etc.). They thought it was a great event to "help" Charlie when a runaway bull had to be chased around the Longman and down our street again. As for me, I felt safer with the front door and the stairs between me and any likely Ferdinand. I was amused to read, later, of the runaway animal which mounted the Stairs in the old "Buttercup Dairy" premises in Hamilton Street.

The boys used to "help" all sorts of people — like the staff at Alan Cobham's Air Circus on the Longman Aerodrome when they came to town and charged 2/6d for an air-flight. My brothers had their share of "looping-the-loop" for nothing, in return for odd jobs around the Aerodrome.

The Ragman was always a welcome visitor to our street. We scrounged around for rags and woollens in exchange for goldfish, balloons and whirring birds or windmills on a gaily coloured stick. Sometimes the exchange rates were cups and saucers . . . very dull alternatives, to our minds!

We had the regular beggars too, called after their line of patter or appearance, e.g. "Spare a Copper" or "Forty Pockets". We were all warned of the consequences of calling after tramps and the like and that we would be gobbled up by bears like the children in the Bible who had called after the Prophet Elijah (or was it Elisha?). That did not deter some of the more impudent boys.

The most colourful characters of all were the buskers who frequented our street. Perhaps it was because it was a long wide street with plenty of room for improvisation and wide pavements for the audience and some of them could put on quite a good show (to our unsophisticated eyes, at any rate).

There was one old couple who regularly toured the street, he with an orange box which he placed down lovingly for his wife to sit on, while he sang in a quavering voice "Rock of Ages" or "In the Good Old Summertime". His wife sometimes joined in with him and they were both a source of inspiration for my young brother and sister, who used to imitate them when playing at home in the evenings.

There was a roly-poly of a "Wee Mannie" who was a wizard on the spoons. He made a "Clackity-clackity click-click" noise all up and down his arms, legs and thighs and then he would turn somersaults, periodically, singing all the time. His forte was, "Oh I wonder, yes I wonder, Will the Angels way up Yonder, Will the Angels play their harps for me?" I wonder!

There was another fellow who "Plonkity-plonk plonked" and twanged his Jews (or Jaws) Harp and another who accompanied his ditties with the cracking of ivory sticks stuck between each of his fingers. One of my brothers used to gather up the soup-leftovers for flank bones which he dried off and then made "Crackers" which he used to play quite successfully.

The busker who annoyed my sister amd me most was the violinist who scraped jerkily at his violin in the early hours of Sunday morning before breakfast, when we were trying to enjoy a long lie. There seemed to be no tune in the sound he was making . . . and yet, later when I came to appreciate music properly, I could detect a faint resemblance in his staccato-like playing to Fritz Kreisler's "Humour-esque". It could be that he was a professional violinist down on his luck.

My own favourite busker was "Cappie" (or "Cackie") Eppie. I think the "Cappie" part must have been a la Invernessian for the hip-length cape she wore over her long black skirt or perhaps the huge golfer's cap she sometimes wore. Her whole appearance, as I remember, resembled that of the "Old Mother Riley" character created for the film of that name around the thirties — but I don't know who copied who! Sometimes she wore a black mutch affair tied with black ribbons under her chin. I cannot remember whether it was a concertina or a melodeon she played on and I cannot remember her playing any particular tune. All I remember was that I could never keep my feet still when I heard her playing and kicking her legs up in time to the music. I got into lots of trouble for scuffing my school shoes, imitating her antics. I was very upset one day to see poor Cappie lying in the gutter face-downwards, clutching her melodeon and I thought she was dead. However, one of the grown-ups who knew all told me not to worry as she was not dead — just dead drunk! Seemingly she had come from a very good family but had become addicted to the bottle.

I don't know what happened to Cappie and the other buskers who came to our street, because we moved away to a new house further away from the town centre. No doubt the Welfare State takes care of most of the Cappie Eppies and Forty Pockets of this generation . . . and yet I've seen the "drop-outs" recently when passing through London and they are just as featured in the song "Streets of London" which my children play on their guitars. They look miserable besides the happy-go-lucky "fellows who don't fit in" of my childhood years.

37

My daughters scream with laughter when I tell them that, even at the age of around twelve, a boy known to us would never pass us in the street without saluting or touching his cap — even if we hated the sight of each other. We just inclined our head slightly, smiled graciously and passed on our way — particularly if either of us were accompanied by a grown-up.

At the School Dance, no-one would stand in front of us, with a hitch-hiking style "thumbs-up" and take it for granted that you knew he was asking you to dance. Such a request was always preceded with a little bow and a "May I?". More hoots of derision when I tell my daughters about the little cards with pencils attached which we wore on our wrists for very special dances. This makes them explode and say that I really must have grown up in the Victorian era. Contrasting present-day standards, I just smile wistfully and think I'd never trade their so-called "with-it" styles for my childhood days of "gracious living", now, alas, gone with the wind!

Tops, hoops and peashooters

I BEGIN with a story I heard the other day. "Sanny", on his return from a visit to the South of England, was asked how he made himself understood. "Och," he said, "'At wis easy. A left oot all 'e Rs and gied 'e words a bit o' chow in 'e middle." Now, here are a few more "Thirsa wordies" to "chow" over:—

Bonnad, Cap; Clash, Gossip; Cloored, Bashed; Deugen, Stubborn; Dorts, Huff; Dunt, Bump; Foosty, Musty; Gant, Stammer; Ganzie, Jersey; Gravvad, Scarf; Geetcher, Grandfather; Ingan, Onion; Lowped, Jumped; Neep, Turnip; Purn, Cotton Reel; Sassengers, Sausages; Semmad, Undervest; Slevver, Dribble; Teet, Peep; Twite, Pare.

The ingenuity children used to show in making their own playthings and amusements was admirable. The shopkeepers had little peace due to the young lads coming in and asking for "any owld carmal tins".

With these tins we'd borrow a pair of scissors ("How did iss scissors get so blunt?"). Our plans were in our heads, our tools were the scissors and a stone. We'd cut the tin and fold it over and batter the edges using the stone as a hammer.

Our end product? — a "boatie".

We then proceeded to "'e holl" behind the breakwater to launch our "boatie". Our first trials may not have been successful (shades of Q.E. II!) but after a bit more hammering at the edges, and perhaps a few pebbles for ballast — "she's floatan' fine now!"

We'd then search around the "holl" for a "bit o' clootie" and a "stickie" and have a sail rigged on our "boatie". When there were no tins available we might use a flat board which we would point at one end (the bow) using a seagull feather as a sail.

"Kerties" were all the rage and, once again, the shopkeepers were the suppliers. Crates from syrup tins were the favourite. We would then "cadge" wheels and axles off an old pram. As there was little traffic we had the run of the roads.

"**Spinning Tops**"? We got the cotton reels from the tailors and "twited" one end to a point. Large numbers of children used to congregate in front of Mrs Norn's shop and the Town Hall which seemed to be a favourite playing area during the dark evenings. (Perhaps, this was due to this area being better serviced with lamplight). Children's games were seasonal but there was always a gathering around Mrs Norn's shop. Yes, we even played football in the square until there came the familiar warning, "Here's 'e bobbies," and we disappeared in seconds!

"**Buttonie**": Perhaps readers will remember that game when we tossed buttons into a chalked circle on the pavement. Some enterprising lads used to make a lead "button" which didn't roll away on landing in the circle and when the opponent had lost all his stock of buttons he was "rooked". (I don't know where that word derived from). We had the usual games of hide and seek. The sounds of the lassagies at their own games, singing like "linties" (linnets) "Celie Celie Walker." "The wind, and the wind, and the wind blows high." I bet that brings back nostalgic memories! We never seemed to feel the cold — changed days — now one sees the young ones "clookan" under duffel coats and anoraks!

"**Hoops**" or "**Girds**" were in great demand at certain times of the year. The more sophisticated would cadge a bicycle wheel, complete with spokes and tyre. "Mac" Mowat was our main supplier. I wonder how "Mac" disposes of them nowadays? We ran miles pushing those wheels.

"**Pea Shooters**": We made our own. This was also seasonal. "Danie" MacAdie used to hire workers for plucking the geese, turkeys, etc., in preparation for the festive season. The lads cadged goose feathers and used the quills as pea-shooters and barley as ammunition. The stock of barley in the homes used to disappear quickly especially if there were a few boys in the family and many mothers found they were short of barley for the broth on a Sunday morning!

We used to buy a pennyworth of rubber tubing from the chemist. This tubing was originally used for the old-type feeding bottles, but trust us, we would find a use for it! We would tie a knot on one end of the tubing and fix the other end to a tap and fill it with water. More often than not the tubing would burst and the operator would be soaked! We just ran around until we dried then presented ourselves as innocent as usual.

"Hingan on 'e Larries": The horse-drawn lorries were plentiful and one would always see the boys "hingan on" until the "bobbies" spotted them. The "boys in blue" seemed to be at every corner and always turned up to "spoil our fun". No doubt it was for our own good, but we liked a chase and if caught we'd get a wallop and should we complain we got another one!

❖❖❖

Thinking back to her childhood, an Alness resident penned this nostalgic verse:

> The porridge supped, the stories told
> When blowing broth to make it cold
> Around our kitchen table.
> The homework done ere set sun
> Then tiddlywinks, oh they were fun,
> Around our kitchen table.
> The cakes mum baked, the bowls we scraped
> The garments sewn, the curtains taped
> Around our kitchen table.
> The jam jars sealed after fruit yield
> Chopped veg from field, the tatties peeled
> Around our kitchen table.

41

We loved picnics in the Longman

AS a child, brought up in Innes Street, Inverness, the name "The Longman" holds many memories for me.

It was our favourite picnic spot and, on a fine day, most of the mothers in the street brought their children there to swim, collect mussels and winkles — or just play around a crackling twig fire until the tea was ready. Of course, in those days, there was only the golf course and airfield and no industrial or other buildings. We could start off from the bottom of Innes Street and walk all around the Longman and come home by the top of the street, without meeting a car.

At night the Longman would become transformed from the bright playground into an eerie, frightening place — particularly near "The Haunted House." This was a ruined dwelling-house near Seafield Farm and probably got its name because it was derelict and the moonlight threw weird shadows from the trees on it. I was too terrified to go near it, even in broad daylight!

I have often wondered about the origin of the name, "The Longman" and wondered if there was any truth in the answer given to me by one of the older girls, when I asked about it. She said that it was so called because there was an outlaw buried there, whose grave stretched all the way round, as he had been so long — hence "The Long Man." She even pointed out a huge stone at the corner of a dyke facing the sea and said that was the gravestone and that a nearby tree was where the outlaw had been hanged.

In later years, when I began to think about it, I wondered if this could possibly have been my Lewis grandmother's bogeyman, namely "Mac an t-Sronaich", a huge gorilla-like man!

We always spent our school holidays on the Island of Lewis and, when we were out of hand, my Granny would always threaten us with "Mac an t-Sronaich."

She told us hair-raising stories of his escapades and said he was a mass-murderer who had lived in a cave near the village and sometimes, when he was hungry, he would come down at night to steal children and EAT THEM!

From what I could gather in later years, there was an Outlaw called "Mac-an t-Sronaich", whose name was supposedly MacKenzie and from the Gairloch area. He had escaped to the Outer Hebrides and had been guilty of several murders in the Lewis/Harris area. Eventually, he was supposed to have been outwitted, captured and hanged and buried in Inverness . . . but where? No-one seems to know, unless, perhaps he was really "The Long Man" . . .

Weird beliefs
in Rosemarkie

AS IN most villages in Scotland with any history at all, there are plenty of old tales still being told and weird and wonderful beliefs still cherished in Rosemarkie even if they come to the surface only when a book like this is being written — or when an old man sits by the fire with his pipe, a dram or two and a young audience.

Round here it is still held that when the Last Day arrives the seat of judgement will be on the Moor of Navity above the Eathie Burn. True this spot is nearer to Cromarty than to Rosemarkie but as in old days Cromarty was the centre of law and order for the district, perhaps it is only right and proper that the final court should be near there. Another story relates that the plans for the cathedrals at Elgin and Fortrose got mixed up by the imps who had been ordered to build them in a single night by the wizard Michael Scot. Having finished this work in good time, Michael had to set them to do more lest he should be torn to pieces himself by the dangerous children of Satan who, if not kept busy, would have destroyed their master. He ordered them to build a mound and on the top a road at the entrance of the Inverness Firth from Ardersier to Chanonry Point. To the imps this was easy and they made good progress with the mile-long job on a moonlight night till a passing Highlander blessed their labour — and that was the end of that.

Not far away from Rosemarkie in Munlochy Bay there is a cave where Finn and his warriors lie entombed — waiting to be summoned by three trumpet calls when they are needed to help their country again. A trumpet was sounded once and the warriors stirred — but so frightful did they look that the trumpeter fled not daring to sound it again and there they still wait — raised on their elbows now — for the trumpet calls that have never come.

Nearer Rosemarkie there are two large country houses each of which is haunted. Flowerburn House by a poltergeist — never seen but always ensuring that any potential intruder suffered dire harm — and Raddery House where the Green Lady walked. No local person would ever walk the low road to Raddery at night for fear of meeting her. But her spirit found rest after a skeleton, found beneath an ancient hearthstone, had been given decent burial.

There are several stories of mysterious disappearances, such as that of the man with his plough and two horses who disappeared suddenly and forever in a shaft above the rocks, a shaft that was said to have been sunk by a prospector in search of coal — or the disappearance of a "wifie" who went looking for a lost lamb in one of the caves along the shore and who was never seen again. A party of men who went to look for her went in to the cave for a considerable distance and still could not find the end of it and discouraged, or fearful, returned to daylight and the beach.

Right up to fairly recent times there was, locally, strong belief in magic and the evil of magic. An old farmer for whom nothing would thrive decided to consult a wise man near Inverness, who took out a pail of clear water, put in first a silver ring and then a gold one and finally a lump of coal from the fire. He stirred all this round for a while, told the farmer to look into the pail and see if he saw a face. He did and saw his neighbour's — he went home, had things out with his neighbour and all went well!

There is a curious pagan connection surely in the old custom, now died out, of carrying lighted torches through the streets on Hogmanay.

Of witches there seem to have been plenty in Rosemarkie at one time or another — perhaps the legends about them have emanated from the story of the Brahan Seer who was burnt in a barrel of tar on the Ness of Fortrose, but not before he foretold the curious doom that was visited on the house of Seaforth. More recently an old crone was said to have put a curse on a man who had "crossed" her. She made a clay model of her enemy and each day she took the model to Rosemarkie Burn and washed it and each day a little of the clay was washed away — till the day came when there was no more clay to wash and on that day he died.

Another story of sudden death is that of the architect who designed and built Fort George for the Hanovarians as a frontier garrison for keeping the wild Highlanders at bay after the '45. He is said to have come across to Rosemarkie to view his handiwork, to have been suddenly smitten with remorse, being a good Scot, for what was implied in his achievement, and to have committed suicide on the spot.

Then there is the tale of the unfilled grave by the Grey Cairn on the hill above Rosemarkie — and the story of the man who, having tired of his sweetheart and found another, enticed her there, meaning to murder her. He was disturbed and she went free and to this day as if in solemn warning, the grave remains open.

But there are happier tales too. Old Bellac — the wifie from Avoch who used to come weekly to Rosemarkie to collect, in the Fairy Glen, material for her herbal concoctions — and the illicit stills that had flourished all round the neighbourhood. There was one at Ardmeanach where, when the Gauger (Exciseman) suddenly appeared, the crofter's wife made his tea with the golden liquid and while he was "out" — knocked senseless, her husband and his friends had been able to hide all the incriminating evidence.

Older folk will chuckle as they remember some of the "characters" of the area — such as the man who announced to his friend "I hear Johnnie Hossack is off to Honomalu (Honolulu) tomorrow; change at Glasgow!" Or Jock Perrish, the first man to fly, who tied himself and baited fish hooks to a stout pole and when the geese, after coming to the bait, flew up in desperate flight, Jock too, was airborne — and geese, and hooks, and pole and Jock "flew" to Artafallie eight miles away, from where he got a lift home!

Then, too, there was Old Kilravock — whom everybody was convinced was a witch and whose house the children always passed at the run. When she wanted to go anywhere, she stood in the road, waved her long stick at the first vehicle to come along and so malevolent did she appear, that even the Queen herself would have stopped and made a place for her in her carriage.

Finally, there is a charm which was said to be effective against anyone possessed of the evil eye, but to be of any use, it had to be spoken in good old Anglo Saxon four lettered words.

Walking barefoot
in the dust

I AM 70 years old and my memory is NOT good but here are a few of the things I remember in my youth.

A great pleasure was to see the various horse buses from Inverness hotels galloping up Fairfield Road to meet the "Glengarry" and the "Gondolier" as these boats arrived at Muirtown, where the hotel porters vied for the passengers to come to their hotel. It was a colourful and exciting sight to see the buses, drawn by two or four horses, and raising dust which settled in long lines on each side of the road where barefoot children loved to walk through the dust.

The net fishers at Friars Shott were another attraction where I have once seen 30 big fish landed in one cast. "Allan" was the children's favourite. He pulled the rope attached to one end of the net from about Celt Street down river and always had several kids helping him. There were children with jam jars catching little eels from under stones at the river's edge and chanting "Needlie, Needlie, knot your tail and you'll get back to your mammie again."

A great achievement was to wade across the river. The bank had not been built up as now and was a very pleasant (if a bit damp) place to play, with lots of wild flowers.

Across the river was the "Maggot Green." Jimmie Johnson — the "Maggot" poet — wrote: "There never was grass that grew so green, as the grass that grew on the Maggot Green." And "Shine on, fair moon, upon the slates and let the fishermen see to catch salmon and skates." And "See the fly upon the steeple looking down on all the people." He was a neat, tidy, little man with a look about him of having been a sailor and I think he was English. He sold us poems — carried in a red and white spotted handkerchief — for one penny each.

I think "Forty Pockets" was so called because of the many coats and jackets he wore. Did he collect clothes for re-selling and find that the easiest way to carry them? I wonder.

In 1914-18 it was "all hands to the plough" and the old Public Park (which boasted a bandstand) was converted into allotments where Park Road now is, were the first of these. It was hard work getting these into trim but we grew grand crops of vegetables there. I think each allotment was 200 yards square. It was pleasant and profitable for allotmenteers to rest occasionally and gather together and swop stories and gardening hints and samples of their produce.

The Americans had a camp beside Carse Farm and a supply boat called "The Black Hawk" moored in the Beauly Firth. They were popular with Inverness girls, for they had large supplies of sweets, etc., which were scarce here and they were generous with these. Alas, this did not go down well with our returning soldiers at the end of the war and resulted in very bad rioting in the town for two days.

A popular place of entertainment was The Music Hall on Union Street and a regular singer at local shows was Mr Donald Dallas. He was drill instructor for schools and he and Mr Lee Fraser (draper, whose shop was next door to The Music Hall) sang duets. Mr Fraser sang soberly and musically and Mr Dallas as comic, in exaggerated Inverness accent.

The Black Isle was an ideal place for a picnic. We loved the ferry boat trip and the elders believed a day across Kessock was a good tonic and a cure for whooping-cough.

A Soldier

of the

KING.

AFTER the War every man who has served will command his Country's gratitude. He will be looked up to and *respected* because he answered his country's call.

The Regiments at the Front are covering themselves with Glory.

Enlist To-day.

At any Post Office you can obtain the address of the nearest Recruiting Office. **Enter your name to-day on the Nation's Roll of Honour and do your part.**

This was a characteristic Great War recruiting advertisement before the introduction of conscription. Alas, the fine-sounding prophecy was far from the bitter reality of 1919.

*Above: One of the few remaining fishermen's thatched cottages at Ardersier.
Below: Castle Stuart, now closed and boarded up . . . but still reputed to
be haunted.   See "Ardersier . . . where ghosts lurk."*

Gas lamps, horse-drawn vehicles and an atmosphere of placid calm characterised Inverness High Street in 1870.

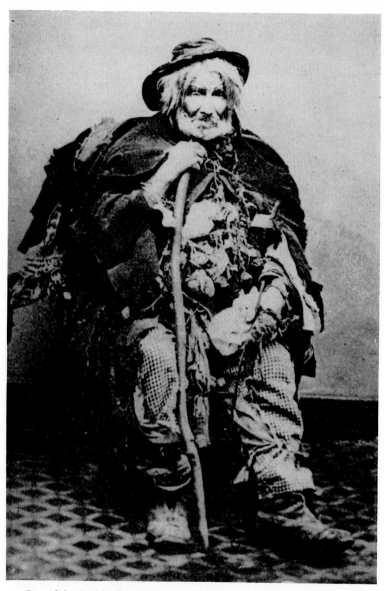

One of the Highland's most notable "characters" in Victorian days was "Forty pockets," otherwise known as Fearquhar A'Shunna. Tales of his eccentricities were legion.

So much
to remember . . .

BEING a nature-lover, my memories of the "long ago" are linked with the passing seasons.

Spring came late in our Northern village, and snow lay in nooks and crevices until February — "Wearan awa" as in the well known "Land o' the Leal". Later, however, primroses carpeted the ground in the silver-birch woods, and as children, we made long pilgrimages to gather huge fragrant branches.

Our cottage home had surrounding trees of great beauty, including a large rowan. Many summer evenings were spent there, enjoying the pleasure of a swing, and I can still remember the scent of the "snowy clusters white". A peat moss lay some distance from the village and there we held competitions in jumping from the highest banks — surrounded by the heather bloom, with its honey-sweet scent. How simple and wholesome were our youthful pleasures!

Autumn brought colour and beauty. We ran guiltily among the corn stooks, and gathered sprays and leaves ranging from lemon to copper. Memories are again awakened of the rowan tree — "so rich and gay its autumn dress wi' berries red and bright."

Hallowe'en — how we enjoyed guising, carrying turnip lanterns round the village. We had our share of village "worthies", some rather awesome to our young minds, but mischief demanded that we visit them! Often we were made welcome — sometimes we made a hasty retreat!

Christmas — almost invariably a white one — crowned the happy year. There were the usual parties, where music was provided by local talent. We wore a new dress, perhaps silver sandals, special gifts, and felt the magic of Christmas! There were services in our local churches, one of which has a special memory of moonlit spruce trees bent blue-shadowed over untrodden snow.

Yes — our youth was happy. I dedicate my memories to parents who toiled cheerfully to provide for our happiness, who shared our joys, and whose own memory still shines on through the passing years.

◆◆◆

Mrs K. Palmer, of Pondfield Road, Dagenham, Essex, has the happiest memories of holidays she spent as a child at Fochabers. She writes: "I can still taste those wonderful buns and baps we bought at the old-fashioned baker's shop at the end of the street. At the other end was a gate leading into the grounds of Gordon Castle. All day a dear old man used to sit at this gate. He was called Sandy and used to let us into the grounds whenever we wished. I was about nine years old at the time and I remember so many happy things like paddling in the burns or walking in the rain in macs and gum-boots through the bracken. My father was wonderful to be with: he knew every bird and wild flower. Maybe I shall one day return to that little street and the gate in the wall. Love of the Highlands is bred in us from our grandparents so I am delighted that my son is now working for the Forestry Commission at Fort Augustus."

New girl made quite a splash!

LET ME tell you about my first day at school. I lived a ten minute walk — five minutes if you ran — from the school. I always did the latter.

Clutching an envelope in my hand I arrived breathless in the infant room. The teacher asked me who I'd like to sit beside; so I pointed to a fair curly-haired girl. Much to my disappointment she pushed me along to sit by a straight-haired boy. Yes, you've guessed it. He was the boy next door.

I got a lined slate and on the top line the teacher made the figure 1 for me to copy. This I laboriously did; and when finished I was told to fold my arms and listen. Fine and easy, as I'd always been a good listener.

At one o'clock I rushed home for dinner followed by my class mate. Coming to a large pool I made to run round it, but he came behind me and pushed me in. He said "As sure as I'm a living sowel that's hoo the lassie broke the boul." My spelling may not be accurate but he didn't pronounce the words soul and bowl. I changed into dry clothes before running back to school for the afternoon. I was then allowed to colour the three beans with crayons.

Coming home at four o'clock I was pursued by a bigger girl who had a long way to go home. She told me that she was a witch and would kill me if I didn't give her a "piece" I got a "piece" from my mother to give to her and that was one witch who disappeared very quickly!

A young boy who had just left school was employed by a crofter who, as he was a bachelor, kept a housekeeper. On a quiet Sabbath

51

afternoon they could always hear kennel dogs barking in the distance. The dogs belonged to the laird of the estate on which there were several large farms and many small crofts.

Anne, the housekeeper, remarked one day, "Oh! what a noise that Spaniards are making." The youth said "They are not Spaniards, Anne, they are spaniels."

"Excuse me, sir," replied Anne, "but I was in school as good as you."

◆◆◆

Stories of the Loch Ness Monster are legion and a separate book would be needed to tell of them all. However, there is only one person who claims to have seen TWO Nessies at the same time! The story is that a retired farmer, Mr Francis Stuart, of Lewiston, was working on his land at Kerrodown when he saw the "monster" appear in the middle of the loch. He stopped to watch it and then was astounded to see a second "monster" surface off Castle Urquhart. Mr Stuart first saw Nessie back in 1927 when he was rowing on the loch and he had a second sighting 30 years later. He described the monster as "a little submarine."

Where the bride hid her children

BIG events in the lives of children at the beginning of this century were the Sunday School picnic and the soiree at Christmas. The picnic took place during the school summer holiday and we used to go to John o'Groats beach, which in those days had beautiful sand. We went in "machines" (dog carts or such-like) whereas the children of another denomination had to go in farm carts and could not go so far. In Sunday clothes, and each carrying a mug, and on our triumphant way, all of ten miles, we cheered and 'hooched' at every passer-by. The tea was made in a big pot, with water boiled over an open peat fire, made on the shore. Maybe it tasted a bit smoky but that just added to the flavour.

When my Grannie was a little girl in a fishing village near Wick, where her father was gamekeeper to the local laird, she and the other youngsters used to go round the houses at Hogmanay, singing:—

> Get up, auld wife and shake your feathers,
> We dinna come to ye as beggars.
> We are but bairnies at oor play,
> We've come to get oor Hogmanay.

The resulting currant bun and oranges and so forth were then taken to one of the parent's houses and a party was held.

I remember my grandmother telling me the story of a man, contemporary with her father, being summoned by the elders of the Kirk for being the father of an illegitimate child recently born to a girl in the parish. He was given a stern lecture by the elders, and told that he would have to pay a fine of half-a-crown, a lot of money in those days. He agreed to pay, but asked first what would be done with the money. "It will be given to the poor of the parish," said the leading elder. "Oh, well," said the culprit, "I'll just take it home to my mother, she's as poor as any in the parish!"

53

My grandmother also recollected a marriage being contracted between two persons of somewhat higher class than the average, and said that during the ceremony the bride had her three young illegitimate children hidden under her ample skirts. Granny did not know, but I believe this was an old Scottish method of legitimising the children.

People were very superstitious in those days. There was little or no lighting, especially in the country areas, so any light seen at night was usually the subject of speculation and discussion. If no logical explanation could be found, the light was held to be a warning, usually of a death.

Much superstition centred around the moon. It was held to be a sign of bad weather if the new moon appeared "with the old moon in her arms," a reference to a common sight in the nocturnal sky when the new moon is bright but a very pale illumination of a greater part may be seen.

At Candlemas Day, 2nd February, the day was supposed to be a "cock's stride" longer than on December 22nd. I think that was about quarter of an hour, but I'm not sure. This saying also appears in other parts of Great Britain.

Cure for a cut
— a spider's web

IN THE years 1918 to 1928 my family moved all over the country and into Inverness-shire. I remember all those flittings well. To us, the children, a flitting was a sheer delight, as we had to sleep on what mother called a "shakedoon." The night before, as the beds were all taken to pieces, and chaff beds were the rule and when new chaff was to be got, a high, comfortable bed was achieved that night.

My mother believed in all the old cures, such as cold tea for eye troubles, and a spider's web to cover a deep cut. — and that was really effective. There must have been some of the mould which in modern times has been used in penicillin. My father belonged to Cromarty and a good man called Davie Ross lived there in other days. Many tales were told about him, and Dad often told us how the Devil was always tempting Davie and would shout in the window "The sheep is in the corn, Davie," just to see if Davie would forget his goodness and swear!

My Dad was walking home one night, and coming near a certain well on a dark road, stopped to light his pipe. The well was supposed to be a favourite haunting place of the Devil. Dad was just in the act of putting a match to the filled pipe when an awful screech sounded just at his ear. He told us his bonnet lifted right off his head. He burnt his fingers, dropped his pipe and fled as if the "deil" was really after him! He realised that it was probably an owl, but going back the next day he could not find his pipe. So he really wondered: did Auld Nick smoke?

Spirit of
the Oykel

AS YOU drop down over the Struie in Ross-shire and see
before you one of the finest panoramas in Europe, beyond Bonar
Bridge lie the river Oykel and Loch Shin. How many, I wonder,
ever pause to consider how those strange names Oykel and Shin
derived? Or, for that matter, Bonar itself? Listen, and I'll tell
you . . .

Long, long ago in the Invershin district there was a massive
castle inhabited by a foreign knight. Some said he had fled from his
own country to escape death for treason; some made other guesses.
Whatever the reason, there he was living in great comfort and surrounded by many retainers. Nearest and dearest to him were his
daughter Bona and his niece Oykel. Both were young and beautiful
— but there the similarity ended. Bona was fair and gentle. Oykel
was dark, haughty and vindictive.

Also in the large household was the young Prince Shin, of
Norway, who was also reputed to have had to leave the country of
his origin in great haste and in mysterious circumstances. He was
handsome and brave, and both Bona and Oykel fell desperately in
love with him. For some time he had the agreeable task of deciding
which of the two he preferred, but eventually he chose the gentle
Bona and he sought her hand in marriage The old knight was happy
to give his consent and all seemed set for a joyful marriage.

Oykel, however, was bitterly disappointed that the prince had
chosen Bona. She brooded upon the imagined slight until disappointment gave place to fierce jealousy and ultimately to hate. She
resolved that her cousin would have to die and thus drive the prince
to turn to her. Accordingly Oykel bribed one of her uncle's
retainers to carry out the deed and in due course he reported that he
had carried out her instructions and had concealed the body in one
of the disused dungeons in the depths of the castle.

Bona's disappearance caused a tremendous set at the castle. The whole district was scoured; rivers and glens were searched; lochs were dragged. All to no purpose. Prince Shin was in despair. He wandered the lonely and deserted countryside in an agony of grief hoping against hope that he would find his young bride. Meanwhile, what of the knight? He racked his brains to find an answer to the mystery. Inevitably his thoughts turned to foul play. But who would have done such a thing? Who could have reason to harm such a sweet and kind girl as Bona? Suddenly suspicion centred on Prince Shin. That was it! He had tired of her and had sought this fearful way to escape from the marriage contract. No sooner had the knight made up his mind than he took action. By his order the prince was seized during the night and thrown into a dungeon . . . the very dungeon, as it happened, into which the body of his bride had been concealed.

Bewildered, angered and grief-stricken, the young prince lay in the darkness unable to believe that life could be so cruel. Lying thus, with his mind in a turmoil, he was startled to hear a low moan somewhere near him. He groped his way in the gloom and came across a figure lying so still that it seemed lifeless. But again there was a faint moan and his first thought was that it was another unfortunate who had incurred the wrath of the knight. He knelt down beside the recumbent creature and then, his eyes becoming used to the darkness, he saw to his amazement that lying before him was the hapless Bona. Bleeding heavily from a terrible stab wound, she was close to death.

He tore his clothes to bind up the wound and frantically did his best to restore her . . . but it was only too evident that there was little he could do in his cold and dark prison. Suddenly the heavy door of the dungeon creaked open and the prince saw in the doorway the figure of Randolph, one of the knight's men, who was only too obviously in the role of executioner. Prince Shin faced the man calmly:

"Come then, Randolph," he said. "Do what you must, but I wish it had been anyone but you. We were good comrades in battle . . ."

But Randolph seemed scarcely to hear the prince. Indeed, he appeared startled to see him in the dungeon at all. "My lord," he exclaimed, "I came to do you no harm. I would never lift a finger against you. No, I came to . . . to . . ." His eyes went to the figure of Bona, and he suddenly covered them with his hands. "I did not know that you loved her or I would never have carried out the terrible order . . ."

Suddenly all was clear to the prince. Seizing the trembling man by the throat he demanded to be told the name of the person who had instructed him to murder Bona. Randolph, sobbing, said that he had been away from the castle on a foraging expedition and knew nothing of the bethrothal of Prince Shin and the lady Bona. On his return he had been sent for by Oykel. She told him that she was engaged to Prince Shin but that Bona, through jealousy, was trying to set the old knight against Shin and had even plotted to poison both her and the prince. Randolph said he believed what Oykel had told him and, being greatly attached to the prince, had at once agreed to carry out Oykel's wishes. He had stabbed Bona and, believing her dead, had hidden the body temporarily in the dungeon until he had an opportunity to remove it and bury it outside the castle.

He had come to the dungeon that day for that purpose not knowing that the prince was also there and certainly not having any reason to believe that Bona was still alive. He pleaded for the prince's understanding and forgiveness and vowed to do what he could to effect his escape. The prince told Randolph he believed he had acted in good faith, and together they worked out a plan of escape. It was soon put into effect and shortly afterwards the prince and Bona were safely concealed and trusted friends of the household came to assist the girl's recovery.

In the meantime, Oykel's hate had given place to frenzy. She had certainly disposed of her rival for the hand of Prince Shin, but now the Prince had disappeared. Everything had gone wrong and she had no-one to turn to. Stung by remorse and in agony of unrequited love, she threw herself into the river which has ever since been called by her name, and is still said to be haunted by her spirit.

Prince Shin and Bona emerged from their concealment, Bona having fully recovered from her terrifying experience. They were reconciled to the knight and after a marriage of great pomp and splendour, sailed away to Norway where, of course, they lived happily ever after.

The loch was named after the prince, and Bonar Bridge, as you have guessed, commemorates the young bride.

True? False? Who knows for sure? But it is a tale worth telling . . . and it certainly adds romance to a drive through this beautiful district.

Pierrots and illuminated fetes

I WAS born in Inverness in 1900. My father was born in Muir of Ord and my mother in Petty. In due time my father became a baker and confectioner and had his own business in Eastgate, Inverness, for many years. His cousin set up a business in Church Street for the sale of hand-made shoes and another cousin was at one time the Provost of Inverness.

My mother had a cousin who became a grocer and eventually owned all the houses in Glebe Street. The one he lived in is still to be seen with a rounded gable. His son went to Tasmania, prospered as a farmer, and at the time of his death was Governor-General.

As a family of three sons and two daughters, we owned a house in Crown Street. As children we were part of a happy community with simple and satisfying pleasures. I recall that we sometimes went into the meal store to see Dan the miller grinding oats, etc. He was always cheery and ready to chat to us. He lived to a good old age in a cottage across the road at the foot of the Brae.

Our local "Bobby", known as "Coronation", was kept busy chasing boys out of back gardens and at other mischief. But he never reported them to their parents — which was a great relief!

When the roads became dry and dusty we jubilantly hailed the local watering cart which sprayed the roads and pavements. We would discard our sandals and follow the cart along the streets getting a delightful drenching. Needless to say there was trouble awaiting us when we returned home soaking wet from head to foot.

The periodic arrival of the pierrots at the public park was awaited with much pleasure. They were known as the Patterson family and were all most talented. Music was played by the local silver band conducted by Mr Tuffy, a silver-haired musical perfectionist. We were so proud of him and the band! There was also the Hungarian band which performed on the Islands from time to

59

time. As a young girl I often would run down the brae to the Islands and listen to what I thought was the loveliest music. There was no doubt that many ladies' hearts were beguiled by those handsome men in their white and gold tunics.

I wonder how many people remember the Illuminated Fetes which were held on the Islands? They were a great pleasure to young and old. The trees were all illuminated with strings of coloured lights; there was splendid music and songs at the Pavilion; and the two platforms were crowded with dancers until midnight. We were both scared and excited when we walked on to the spring bridges on our return home. The men would jump and enjoy seeing the ladies trying to keep their balance as the bridges swayed.

There is another musical memory: the successful concerts arranged by Stuart Roddie at the Music Hall in Union Street. As a young girl I recall a large bus collecting the well-known artistes from their homes. How I enjoyed the glimpse we got of ladies in their lovely dresses and men in Highland evening dress.

And here is a memory which will sound strange, indeed, to the modern generation. We children would hear the sound of a bugle from Annfield Road. "The tourist coach!" we would exclaim — and run to the roadside. The passengers and we would wave to each other and the coachman would again give us a resounding blast on his bugle. We would watch the coach and four horses disappear into the distance and hope that, one day, we too would ride on a coach. But the 1914 war came later and changed our way of living.

Potato holidays in Lochaber

HOW we schoolboys hailed with delight "potato holidays" at the turn of the century in Lochaber. Fourteen happy days away from the tyranny of "sums and strap!" Potato plantings were field days in the crofters' and our childish lives.

Before planting, the crofter hired a pair of horses, with ploughman, at £1 per 12-hour day. The first half-day was spent putting out the manure which was coped in cartloads on each side of a half-acre field. The ploughman, crofter and one or two hefty neighbours carried out this arduous task — up to the knees in glaur and muck!

The busy housewife sent Shonnie or Annag hurriedly for the extra messages required for potato planting day. Among the necessities were a big bag of baker biscuits at eight a penny; cheddar and gouda cheese at 8d and 6d a pound; a 2-pound stone jar of best jam at 8d; an extra half-pound of tea at 1s. The man of the house went for the indispensable bottle of Dew of Ben Nevis whisky: 3s 6d! This amount, calculated in the money values of those days meant a 12-hour day's work.

Next, around 2 p.m., a sort of bush telegraph summoned a team of helpful neighbours, the women and bigger lassies wearing bag aprons to hold the "splits" which had been cut days before. Men and boys arrived carrying graips of various sorts and sizes, ready to shake the manure into the drills. The ploughman opened up the ground, and in every third furrow the ladies deposited the seed 12 inches apart. Men and boys followed carrying large graipfuls of manure to cover the spuds — the boys staggering under the loads as they hurried to beat their elders and be first at the drill, as it was a crime to stop the horses and so start the ploughman's choicest gaelic phraseology!

A self-appointed overseer, generally a crabbed old fellow, followed the squad keeping an eagle eye open for "blanks" or prodding back with his foot any furrow off the straight. All worked at top speed so as to have a breather at the end of the furrow while we waited for the horses to come round for the third time.

Here the youngsters had a few minutes' fun; the older men leaning on their graips and talking weather, crops and the merits or demerits of Kerr's Pink, Champion or Skerry Blues. The boys teased the girls about unlikely lads — as boys will — to annoy them. I remember in particular one lassie, Murag, who concealed a fat worm in her hand and retaliated by dropping it down a cheeky boy's open shirt. Everyone laughed except the victim. He squirmed!

At half-time the crofter's wife retired to the kitchen to bring forth refreshments for the team. Every man got a generous dram (the ploughman two) before his cuppa, but most of the ladies being T.T., they got tea with baker biscuits or Abernethys with cheese. At the finish, about 6.30 p.m., all had developed voracious appetites. A bountiful table was all ready spread and groaned under loads of boiled eggs, toasted oatcakes, quarter-inch thick griddle scones, cheese, jam and fancy biscuits. The bottle was again brought forward by the man of the house. The ploughman got a double, and a bumper to all who took one. The boys were omitted from this solemn ceremony and warned of the sinfulness of taking drams when too young.

In some cases when there was a fiddler or piper in the team, an impromptu ceilidh and hop followed. In every case there was always a running, cheerful chatter and jokes all round in the gaelic tongue.

This happy communal potato planting in Lochaber and elsewhere gradually died out. Horses and potato teams became fewer and fewer until latterly the few crofters left who planted potatoes had to get the services of a tractor driver and the seed dibbled in — a tame, unromantic potato day holiday!

Nicknames that linger on

Many of us have had to go through life with a "nickname" or "by-name" as we used to call it. Some have been handed down from a parent's nickname, from our school days, or perhaps a physical disability. Maybe it was a pet name used at home until it had been overheard by an outsider.

I think, during our school days, practically everyone had a nickname. To mention a few: "Bo"; "Corky"; "Cheetah"; "Despy"; "Darky"; "Frenchie"; "Henner"; "Inkie"; "Ketchie"; "O'ms"; "Sleeper"; "Skipper"; "Sho-Sho"; "Scooter"; "Smick"; "Piper"; "Uncle" — just a few of the scores of names which come to mind, and are no doubt recognised by many. Some of these nicknames belong to people who are now in distant parts of the world. Perhaps they have forgotten them themselves, but this should jolt their memories.

One well-known councillor in Caithness received his nickname during his football days. Dashing up the wing during a football game, W. S. Smith was christened "Morton", no doubt after that great football internationalist Alan Morton. Years after, he still received the odd letter addressed to him as W. Morton Smith! Another lad, who would dash along the dusty, gravelled playground, then skid to a halt putting the "stoor" about him, was called "Dirt Track Dedge" after some speedway rider, now long forgotten. After over 40 years that nickname still stuck. Another nickname was "O bee" Gunn — this was gained from a circus sword-swallower who had visited the town! Another — "Jura" — probably came about because he came from the island of that name off the west coast of Scotland.

Our teachers did not escape either. Here are just a few of their nicknames: "Sloop", "Chops", "Meek", "Tip-Toes", "Chalker", "Grannie".

During the visits of the Wick people — perhaps to a football match or on an annual holiday — they would be met with cries of: "Week-a-Butta", "Crack-a-Cuppa" to which they would reply with disdain: "Thirsa Soor Sellags!" How interesting it is to try to find the derivation of those names.

In Melvich and the surrounding areas where there are so many families with the same surname one has to make distinctions such as "Red" Mackay perhaps relating to the colour of his hair or perhaps his stature. Most of these nicknames are taken for granted and the recipients probably wouldn't answer to their proper names.

Elegant carriage and pair at Balmoral Lodge, Strathpeffer, in the days when the spa was attracting the nobility and gentry from all over Britain.

CABINET PORTRAIT

More than a mere bike, the "penny-farthing" was a considerable status symbol — as this studio picture indicates.

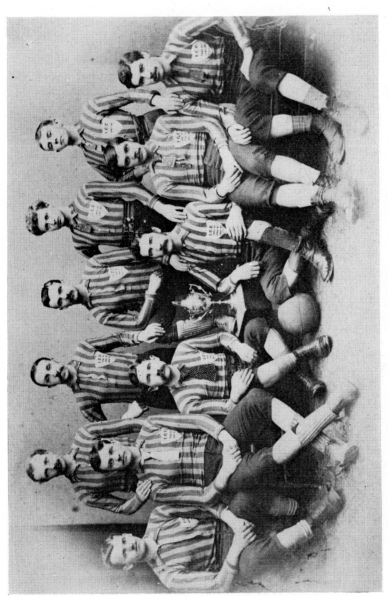

Cup-winners of 1887 — the Inverness Crown football team. Note the knee-breeches and neckties.

Many old people still speak with affection of Willie Roddie's musical and operatic productions at the Inverness Music Hall. This picture is of the company of "Yeoman of the Guard."

"Noah" changed a girl's life

THE Sabbath was truly a day of suppression and depression in my far-off childhood and teenage years. Sunday school twice; church services twice; and finally Bible class: a total of five religious attendances every Sunday, beginning at noon and ending at eight-thirty in the evening. The repression and solemnity have left such a lasting memory that I have forsaken orthodox religion and become a Humanist.

I remember so vividly when I was barely eight years of age being slapped and humiliated for daring to laugh at one of the Sunday school superintendent's stories. To laugh on the Sabbath was as heinous a crime as heresy and here is an account of my fall from grace.

The superintendent was, in our youthful eyes, an old man with a long white beard and short, thick, greying hair, dressed in sober black and with a stern, humourless expression. We called him Noah because he seemed to fit the role perfectly. No-one dared smile, fidget or talk while Noah held the stage. His fanatical eyes swept the hall quelling his pupils into mute submission.

On this particular Sunday school session we were all sitting on the usual hard-backed forms, quiet and attentive when Noah mounted the platform warning us about the wrath to come and the wages of sin. His story on this occasion was Rahab and the scarlet cord and how she was to hang the cord from her window so that the lives of her family would be spared. Then he went on to inform us that Rahab didn't wear skirts or dresses but knickers which he pronounced as knee-kers. I had a mental picture of Rahab in her knickers hanging out a scarlet cord. I was too young to realise the significance of the colour red at a woman's window, but I imagined any woman hanging out of a window dressed only in her knickers was funny, especially dangling a red string, and I laughed at the idea.

65

6

Down came Noah from the platform, like an avenging angel, slapped me across the face with his leather-hard hand, shook me, pulled me out and sat me on the empty side of the hall for all to witness the price of levity at so sacred a tale. On looking back at his behaviour and remembering that he was a bachelor I wonder why he chose such a story for young children. Did my laughing anger him at what was hidden under the knickers and all his pent-up inhibitions find an outlet on the assault? A psychologist would have the answer.

❖❖❖

"Forty-pockets" was a familiar character in Inverness before the second Great War. The curious name was given because this man, educated and reputedly of good family, roamed the streets clad in several coats one on top of the other. All were unbuttoned so that the layers could be marvelled at and the multiplicity of pockets guessed at.

He was also known as the "Railway tramp" because he very often walked along the railway lines. This eventually proved to be his undoing, for he was struck by a train and died from his injuries.

66

Strange noises
on the stairs

One night, in my grandmother's home, the household was awakened by a commotion like people stumbling up and down the stairs. Grandfather got out of bed to see what had caused all the noise, but saw nothing and heard nothing. He went back to bed and, shortly after, the commotion was repeated. All of us wondered what was happening . . . but in time we forgot about it.

Weeks afterwards my mother's brother was drowned in the canal near Inverness. Owing to the narrowness of the lobby, the bearers carrying home his coffined remains had to step backwards up the stairs to place the coffin in a convenient room. Immediately the night's disturbance came to mind. On the day of the funeral a number of mourners had to stand on the stairs. Again, a repetition of the noisy happening. Strange, but true.

Another time a neighbour's baby died. My father, a joiner, made the coffin. A rather wide ditch lay between both houses. Late one night my mother called father to see "a blue starry light on the surface crossing the ditch." When the night came to deliver the coffin, my father crossed over the ditch **first** . . . and mother handed over the coffin.

The last of the Lochaber weavers was a bachelor, Donald MacMillan. He came regularly to our house on Ceilidh. Returning home one night he saw three blue/green orbs emitting from his bedroom chimney. The omen was known as "an sanus." There came the day in 1900 when a neighbour's six-year-old lassie lit a whinbush. Her clothing caught fire and, all alight, she ran to the weaver's house to collapse. Her charred remains were placed in the room . . . from which had come the sanus.

Our Calvanistic elders frowned on card-playing and particularly associated the ace of spades with the Devil. One evening, playing a game with some pals, the dealer dared anyone to walk around the house three times with the ace of spades in his hands. No-one took up the challenge, for it was well known that on the third circuit one would come face to face with the Devil. The challenge put a damper on the game and we went home very apprehensively.

There were all manner of taboos on the Sabbath . . . and not all of them have died out! Shaving was forbidden. So was writing. I remember as a lad wandering in the barn one Sabbath and cutting my toe on something sharp. I got no sympathy from my mother. Wrapping a clootie around the bleeding toe, she commented: "That's what **you** get for playing on the Sabbath."

It was colder in those days!

WHEN we were young we prayed for heavy snowfalls and severe frost, which gave us the opportunity for sledging, snowball fights and slides.

The favourite sledging area in Thurso was from the Princes Street end of Castlegreen Road, past the railway station entrance and down "Lovers' Lane". This is now impossible, owing to the traffic on the roads, but in those days we had plenty of scope. There were many cuts and bruises for those who failed to take the turn on to Janet Street and were suddenly halted by the dyke of Shrubbery Bank! A few of the lads owned the poshest of sledges but the majority made their own. The runners were made by the blacksmiths for a few pence. Incidentally, many schoolboy romances emanated from these escapades in "Lovers' Lane" — How appropriate!

At times when the river was frozen over we would spend a lot of time around the "Factor's Pool" below Shrubbery Bank. We would be happy sliding around and perhaps there would be a few proud owners of ice-skates who would give us a demonstration and perhaps give us a "shottie." It is a long time since I saw the river frozen and strong enough to walk over and the young ones tend to disbelieve us and think we exaggerate.

I have been told by older friends that they remember the frost was so severe one year that the river was frozen and people were able to skate all the way up-river to Halkirk! There were a few enterprising people who had braziers burning and did a roaring trade in the sale of roasted chestnuts.

I have often heard of the people in rural districts being snowed-up for days — perhaps weeks — with "fans", drifts, reaching to the eaves of their cottages. How had they survived? "Och, there was aye something in 'e meil girnal and we always hed wur firkin o' herrin' an' wur tatties. We managed fine." They seemed to be prepared for a few days' isolation and even although their financial circumstances were poor, they survived. When I was employed in a grocer's shop these people bought their goods in bulk. Flour was sold to them by the quarter or half boll.

Castletown to Thurso road would be blocked, but the goods carrier, Jimmie Sutherland, would, instead of using his horse-drawn lorry, bring out his horse-drawn sledge and get the foodstuffs through to the appreciative villagers. We in the town didn't have so much difficulty. The North of Scotland Shipping Company had a vessel making a weekly call to Scrabster with goods and of course the railway was kept open.

During the severe frosty weather we would go down to the small caves opposite the "Clio" The icicles would be about two feet in length. We would have our games of "swash-buckling" using the icicles as swords.

Remember the Bona Ferry?

IT WAS not all that long ago when a half-penny ferry plied between Bona, on the east bank of the Ness a mile or two south of Inverness, and the opposite shore . . . although "not all that long" depends very much on how old you are!   Bona is at the northern extremity of Loch Ness and there was actually a lighthouse for the benefit of the ferry crew.

Sunday was a particularly busy day for the ferry, for many people from Abriachan and the dwellings scattered in that area drove their horses, carts, ponies and traps down to the ferry, crossed the water and then made their way to the Wee Free kirk a little farther on to the east.   They were the lucky ones, of course.   The less fortunate had to make their way on foot — and they included the considerable number of orphans from Glasgow who lived in and around Abriachan with the crofters.

The church used to pay the half-penny ferry fares, for a half-penny was a not inconsiderable sum in those hard days.   The service was very long, what with the Gaelic service, the English service, the Gaelic tables and the English tables.   For those who had come from Abriachan it meant the best part of a day to attend church and the hour was late before they got anything to eat.

Bona was a busy and bustling place in the early part of the century and most times there was a double row of drifters and fishing boats laid up there.   During the Great War security was strictly enforced.   Every man, woman and child for miles around Inverness was issued with a form of passport and was challenged by soldiers posted at all the exit roads and at the canal and loch ends.   Sometimes the military would check all bus passengers.

The Royal Engineers sited a pontoon bridge near Bona with the intention of providing an emergency crossing if the bridge at Inverness were destroyed.   Old people will tell you that the only time that

71

pontoon bridge was used was when a local child tripped across it in high glee! A sight which now seems incredible is recalled by a Black Isle man. It was of the coal shipments from Muirtown to Foyers, commonly of about 100 tons. If there was wind enough, then the shipment sailed slowly past Bona and on to Foyers. If there was no wind, then the shipment went by even more slowly . . . towed by a dinghy with two oars!

Looking down on Bona and the end of the loch from its commanding position 800 feet above sea level, Abriachan is a fascinating community rooted in the distant past but very much alive to the needs and demands of the present. There are records of continuous habitation from prehistoric days and as far back as the 6th or 7th century there was a small settlement of the Celtic Church at Killianan on the shore of Loch Ness. The early missionaries of St. Columba who worked there soon put the land to good use and passed on their considerable knowledge of husbandry to the local people.

Understandably in an ancient place such as Abriachan much of the folk lore still lingers to this day. Even in this age of space ships and moon landings, there are some among the older people of Abriachan who would rather not pass Loch Laide after dark. And there is still suspicion that evil spirits can move in if one is not careful . . . and who is to say this is absurd when, early in 1975, we read of the horror of murder and insanity linked with exorcisms practised in twentieth century England? An Abriachan woman says she can well remember a man walking in silence for 50 miles to Speyside to seek the assistance of the one person he believed could rid him of an evil spell. She can also remember when a cockerel was buried alive under the doorstep of a house, where lived an epileptic child, in the hope of a cure.

Not far away lived a woman who was gifted with second sight and would see the funeral procession of someone about to die — a gift (if that is the appropriate term) which seems to have been shared by many in the Highlands, for such tales are almost commonplace. So numerous are these accounts that they cannot lightly be discounted. Why are none heard about present-day folk? Perhaps because we are moving away from nature itself.

Something which plainly belongs to the world of fantasy is the tale told of the witch of Abriachan who incurred the enmity of her counterpart in Dores, on the other side of the loch. Harsh words, incantations and spells having no effect, so it is said, they started hurling boulders at each other. One thrown by the witch of Dores fell short . . . and can be seen to this day in the water. Not so long ago it was put to good use as a lookout point to spot the steamer from Fort Augustus.

Like a good many other places in the Highlands, Abriachan had a flourishing illicit still industry. Some will tell you it still has! Be that as it may, the difficult terrain made it an ideal place to carry on such illegal processes in comparative security. A notable figure of the past was Duncan Fraser, known and renowned as the King of the Smugglers. Time after time he eluded the excise men and used a score of ingenious methods to outwit them, hide his equipment and cover his tracks. Once, hard pressed, he is said to have disguised his father as a corpse, laid him out on a table in his cottage, put the tell-tale cask in his hand and covered him with a sheet!

The law-breakers did not always come out on top, however. It is recorded that in 1823 during a particularly energetic campaign by the authorities, 400 people in the area were caught and were each fined 20s for illicit distilling and four guineas for selling without licences. It is interesting — and significant — to add that although very tempting bribes were offered for informers there is no known case of a bribe having been accepted. Some say this was because it was such a close-knit community that it would have been unthinkable to betray a friend or neighbour. Others hold that no-one would dare to betray anyone for fear of the punishment which would inevitably follow!

The cinema usher carried a cane!

IN OUR younger days we were avid cinema fans — we never missed Saturday matinees. Our favourite films were "cowboys" and "cops and robbers". In those days of the silent films we were entertained to classical music on the piano by our school music teacher who "thundered" that piano during the exciting parts. We cheered the "goodies" and booed the "baddies". I remember one day a number of the "patrons" smuggled snowballs in to the picture house and pelted the screen when the "baddies" came into view! Roy Munro was employed in the Picture House at that time. He used to have a small cane with which he controlled the boisterous youth. I am sure "Ro-ey" cultivated his first grey hairs during his employment in the Picture House.

I don't know if it was "our gang" or the cowboy films which gave the local lads the idea of forming gangs (don't get the idea that this was like those which are accorded much publicity nowadays). There were "gangs" from different areas — "Up 'e Tooners", "Boorag-Tooners", "Fisher-Beegners" and later the "Glebites". The formation and activities were during the dark nights. We were all good pals during school hours and our battles were arranged as if they were football matches! The word would go around "Wur fachtan 'e Fisher-Beegners 'e nicht, at 7 o'clock."

The "Boorag-Tooners" had their headquarters in an old house — now demolished — at the bottom of Beach Road or at "Tewksie's' garage, midway along Durness Street. All were armed with sticks, "crobbies" or such like weapons. We'd meet the enemy — the "bravest" shouting "charge" came up in the rear!

The "battles" didn't last long before one or the other gang would flee and keep going until they were in their own territory! More time was spent in the preparation. Should a "bobby" come on the scene we all turned tail and dashed away in the same direction. (Ah, well, we live to fight another day!)

Some times the "Boorag-Tooners" would combine with the "Fisher-Beegners" and do battle with the "Up 'e Tooners". I never remember any serious casualties — only a few bruises, but I did feel sorry for one — Johnnie Newlands — who was knocked out. He was soon revived when some bright spark got a large tin of stagnant water from a barrel and threw it over Johnnie. Poor chap! He was more in danger of drowning than suffering ill effects of that crack on the head!

The Gondolier
of happy memory

LAST September at the canal I'd seen the pleasure boat with a load of passengers looking as if they were enjoying their trip — but oh what memories that brought to my mind! I thought of Mac-Brayne's Steamers — the Glengarry, Gairlochy and the Gondolier, but the greatest of these and the longest-lasting was the Gondolier: Paddles, lashing the water behind her and shining with paint and polish. Not only was she ornamental, she was useful and, indeed, necessary as all passengers, mail, furniture, bags of potatoes and peats and indeed the odd sheep were carried as this was then the only means of public transport between Fort Augustus and Inverness. It meant a long day for mothers but it had to be done to get stores and clothe the family for School and Church.

She left Fort Augustus daily at 7 a.m. and called at Invermoriston on the North side; then crossed the loch and collected from Foyers and Inverfarigaig; back again over to Temple Pier serving a wide Glenurquhart — along the same side to Abriachan and crossing again to Aldourie — loading the bits from Dores and district. She centred the loch then and ran for the narrows of the canal at Bona Lighthouse. She was a bonny sight, still lit up in the winter when she arrived there and in spite of the light still burning in the Lighthouse. Sometimes the fog and mist were so thick that Capt. John MacDonald was obliged to halt engines and sound his siren. The lighthouse keeper or any of his family with enough breath had to blow a horn (and what a horn, supplied for that purpose by the late Mr Eustace Porter, the then manager of the canal). This was answered by the steamer siren and was repeated till, by judging distance and direction, the captain found his bearings and blew twice to let us know he was entering the narrows. He never missed!

A short straight run through the made canal ended with Darrich Islands on the right and Castle Spiritane (or Spiritual) on the left.

76

The mound is still there and although large trees have grown all round the base — the table top has never taken a stray seed — it is smooth grass.

On then to the last port and call for collection — Dochfour pier — no sign of it remains. Indeed, from both sides it's stance is inaccessible with bourtie and whins, broom and nettles. But it was there and had a fine double waiting room with scrubbed floor and no writing on the walls! We were handed on to the boat as V.I.P.'s. There our baggage was taken care of by a crewman with "Mac-Brayne's" knitted into his navy blue jersey and "Care of Passenger Luggage" knitted into the back. Capt. MacDonald and his mate and purser wore a navy uniform. Brass buttons, white cap and appropriate number of rings on their sleeves. Our first stop was for the slot machine, where on pushing in $\frac{1}{2}$d. we were rewarded with a sizeable bar of chocolate or Sharpe's Super Cream Toffee decorated with the wee man with the monocle. This was done and probably eaten by the time we passed Dochfour House and Gardens on our left. On then to Dochgarroch locks — passing through seemed such a waste of precious time. The lockmen, helped by the crew, had at that time to open the locks by pushing long poles fixed into an enormous screw on both shores. Through the canal was slow and the scenery much of a sameness — pitching and bushes. So this was our chance to "do the engine room." It shone with brass and steel (and probably, when I think now, with grease) and huge pipes pumping and fitting into larger ones with a rhythm as quiet and regular as the ticking of a clock.

As we slowed down at Muirtown locks, a row of horse-drawn cabs awaited with their drivers running along the edge of the quay waving their whips and trying to catch the eye of passengers into town. There was plenty time for shopping and a short visit to relatives and we left again at 4 p.m., longing then to get home. At the various piers on the return journey the men of the house met the steamer with horse and cart or barrow according to the distance to collect the stores from the Glasgow Shop and boots, etc.

All this is of long ago, but I think it is one of the very few memories of which it can truthfully be said "Oh for the good old days."

Beware
the seals!

IN THE tourist season John o' Groats is a lively, animated place with visitors from all over the world congregating at the accommodation centres and the shops and agreeably conscious of the fact that they are on the most northerly tip of the mainland. But when the last car and the last coach have moved down the road to the south and peace and solitude return to the strange, mysterious Caithness countryside, John o' Groats becomes once again the withdrawn and almost eerie repository of tales and legends told and retold down the ages. One of the most persistent of the John o' Groats folk-tales concerns a seal catcher. This is how it goes . . .

The seal catcher lived not far from John o' Groats House. He did not, of course, specialise only in seals; he went after fish of all sizes and kinds. Nevertheless seals were high on his list of priorities because of the good price he could obtain for their skins. What he did not know, however, was that seals were neither fish nor animals but . . . fairies. One day he made this discovery in a fantastic and unexpected way.

A stranger called at his cottage and said he represented someone who wished to enter into a contract for the purchase of a great quantity of seal skins. The matter was an urgent one and he asked the seal catcher to go with him at once to discuss the deal. Happy to think that he had an opportunity to make a good bargain, the seal catcher agreed to waste no time and climbed up behind the stranger on his big and powerful horse. Off they went at a tremendous pace and in due course came to the edge of a towering cliff at the seashore.

The seal catcher looked around him but could see no-one. "Where is the person you spoke of?" he asked.

"You'll see him soon enough," replied the stranger, and grasping the seal catcher around the waist leapt with him over the edge of the cliff.   They plunged into the sea far below and sank down and down until the seal catcher lost consciousness.

When he regained his senses he discovered to his amazement that he was in a huge room filled with seals, all of whom spoke and felt like human beings.   He was more astounded to realise that he, too, had the appearance of a seal.   Not unnaturally he was deeply distressed by this incredible turn of events but as he was mournfully contemplating his unhappy state he became aware that the seals, too, were in a melancholy mood.   They consoled him with assurances of his personal safety, but he was not too convinced when one of them approached him with a huge knife.

Believing that his life was in danger, he fell down and implored the seals to show him mercy.   Quickly they reassured him and urged him to remain calm.

"Did you ever see this knife before?" asked the stranger who had plunged over the cliff with him.

The seal catcher instantly recognised it as his own knife which, earlier that day, he had stuck into a seal which had then eluded him and escaped.   There was no sense in denial.

"Yes," he replied to the stranger.   "That is my knife."

"Ah," said the stranger.   "Well the seal which you attacked with it is my father.   He is now dangerously ill and only you can save his life.   That is why I had to use deception to bring you here, and I trust you will forgive me."

The incredulous seal catcher was then taken into an inner chamber where he saw the seal he had stabbed that morning.   There was a large and deep wound in its side.

"Place your hand upon the wound and say after me the words I utter," commanded the stranger.   Tremblingly the seal catcher covered the wound with his hand and falteringly repeated the meaningless words which the stranger spoke.   Instantly the wound was healed and the seal arose in perfect health.   As he did so the air was filled with the sound of rejoicing, laughter and happiness.   The seal catcher gazed around him in astonishment and he had the deepest apprehension that now his usefulness was past he would be swiftly despatched.   He gloomily reflected that there was little else that he could expect, for had he not devoted his life to capturing and killing these strange creatures.

Noticing his mournful expression, the stranger approached him. "Do not be disheartened," he said.   "We promised you that no harm shall befall you so you are in no danger.   You had to be brought to our fairy home because only a human hand can cure an

79

ill that had a human cause. You have performed that service and we are grateful. Now you are at liberty to return to your wife and family, but there is one condition. You will be set free only if you give a solemn promise never to maim or kill a seal throughout the rest of your life."

The seal catcher wasted no time in giving his word and gladly went through the ceremony which made the oath binding. Then the stranger took his hand, led him back to the sea-bed and swam up to the surface. As they reached the shore the stranger again uttered curious words and cries and he and the seal catcher were once more transformed into human shape. Mounting the horse which was waiting for them, they thundered back along the road to the seal catcher's cottage. The stranger set him down and without a backward glance raced off to the sea again.

His mind in a turmoil, the seal catcher opened the garden gate and made his way to the door. On the doorstep he saw a large, iron-bound chest. Opening the clasp and throwing back the lid he was stupefied to see that the chest was filled to the brim with gold. He was a rich man and would never need to work again as long as he lived.

Certainly he would never need to catch a seal. He might have been a man of his word . . . but the fairies were taking no chances!

Evocative of days of unhurried travel and leisurely living, this picture shows one of the much-loved paddle steamers that plied up and down Loch Ness.

Riverside horse fairs were red-letter days in Inverness in the nineteenth century. This photograph was taken in 1894.

Theatre=Royal, Inverness.

Mr WELSH respectfully begs leave to inform the Nobility, Ladies, and Gentlemen of Inverness, and its vicinity, that he has engaged Mr RYDER and Mr WILLIAMS for Six Nights, who will make their second appearance this Evening.

On FRIDAY Evening, SEPTEMBER 8, 1826,

Will be performed the Great National Drama of

Rob Roy Macgregor,

OR,

AULD LANGSYNE.

THE PART OF ROB ROY BY MR RYDER.

Rashleigh Osbaldistone, Mr MULLENDER—Francis Osbaldistone, Mr SPANKIE.
Dougal Creature, Mr HOWARD.—Major Galbraith, Mr ANGUS.—Mr Owen, Mr FILLAN.
Captain Thornton, Mr SKINNER.—M'Stuart, Mr THOMPSON.—Saunders Wylie, Mr ROBERTSON
Andrew Fairservice, Mr HART—
Hamish, Miss M. MULLENDER.—Robert, Miss H. MULLENDER.

THE PART OF BAILIE NICOL JARVIE, BY MR WILLIAMS.

Diana Vernon, Mrs SKINNER.—Mattie, Mrs WELSH.—Jean M'Alpine, Mrs FILLAN.
Helen M'Gregor, Miss MULLENDER.

AT THE END OF THE PLAY

A COMIC SONG, BY MR HOWARD.

COMIC SONG, "THE LAIRD O' COCKPEN," MR FILLAN.

To conclude with the laughable Farce of

LOVE A LA MODE,

OR, THE

HUMOURS OF THE TURF.

Sir Archy Macsarcasm, Mr WILLIAMS.—Squire Groom, Mr ANGUS.
Sir Callighan, Mr WELSH.—Beau Mordecai, Mr HOWARD.—Theodore, Mr FILLAN.
Charlotte, Miss MULLENDER.

Doors to be opened at half-past Six o'clock, and performance to begin at Seven o'clock precisely.
Half-price at half-past 8 o'clock.—Children under 12 years of age to be admitted to the Boxes and Pit at Half-price.

Boxes, 3s.—Pit, 2s.—Gallery, 1s.

Tickets and places for the Boxes to be had at Mr Lusk's, Bookseller.

The celebrated Comedy of PAUL PRY is in Rehearsal, and will speedily be Performed.

Inverness: Printed at the Journal Office.

The drama "Rob Roy Macgregor," a farce "Love a la Mode"; and comic songs in the interval provided an excellent evening's entertainment at Inverness Theatre Royal on Friday, 8 September, 1826. Prices: Boxes, 3s, pit, 2s, gallery, 1s.

Something like 100 years ago, this four-in-hand provided a regular twice-daily service between Inverness and Culloden.

Six men were enough

THE river Findhorn, which rises in the Monadhliath Mountains and flows through some of the most remarkable country in the Highlands, is linked with some spectacular events — not least the astounding floods which have occurred along its length from time to time causing much devastation. At Randolph's Leap, two or three miles south of Forres, for instance, there is a stone marking the height reached by the flood waters on one memorable occasion. Looking at the river flowing at the foot of the deep gorge there in normal circumstances, it is almost impossible to believe that the flood not only filled the gorge but flooded the land 30 or 40 feet above it. But it did . . . and perhaps it will again.

However, this is not a story about the attractions of the Findhorn, although one is tempted to digress to describe its spectacular journey from Alpine to Lowland scenery through the valley of Strathdearn. This is a story connected with a rebellion of '45.

Not far from the church of Moy, in the Forest of Strathdearn, there is a singular hollow surrounded by towering rocks and accessible only through a narrow entrance. This was used as a place of concealment for their families by Highlanders in bygone days when they were away on predatory excursions — and it was the scene of a strange and amusing incident at the time of Culloden.

Before the battle, Prince Charlie stayed at Moy Hall as the guest of Colonel Ann, as Lady Mackintosh was called. The Chief had taken the Royalist side leaving his wife to embrace the cause of the Prince, for whom the clans were already gathering. Mackintosh himself was away in Ross-shire but his wife enthusiastically set about raising some 400 of her husband's clan and supporters to rally to the side of the Prince.

81

That Prince Charles was at Moy Hall with Colonel Ann was well known to the Earl of Loudon who was at that time in occupation of Inverness with his troops. He decided to move on Moy Hall to surprise the Prince, and discussed the tactics with his fellow officers over breakfast. One of the girls waiting table overheard them, stole away and ran barefoot to Moy Hall, 12 miles distant, to warn the Prince.

Naturally he was grateful for the warning, but the news caused consternation at the Hall for at that time there were no troops available to defend it. But the consternation did not spread to the redoubtable Colonel Ann. She summoned a council of war from the few men available to her and quickly made plans to deal with the menace of Loudon's force of 1,500.

Donald Fraser, the Chief's blacksmith, afterwards known as the Captain of the Five, at once left his forge. Taking with him five of the Hall staff armed with sword and musket, they set off at the double for that place of concealment not far from the church of Moy. They reached it in the early evening and took up positions where they could watch the approaches without being detected. Scarcely had they settled down for the watch when they heard the muffled sounds of the advancing enemy.

Biding his time, Fraser waited until the soldiers were within 100 yards of them. Then he shouted a command at the top of his voice: "The Mackintoshes, the Macgillivrays, the Macbeans to form instantly the centre; the Macdonalds on the right; and the Frasers on the left." The command was taken up from man to man in a loud voice along a distance of a quarter of a mile, and accompanied by the firing of muskets from each of the six.

Thrown into confusion by this unexpected turn of events and believing that they were confronted by masses of Highlanders in positions of unassailable tactical advantage, the Royalist commander decided to cut and run before his whole force was decimated and routed. He gave the order and the whole force of 1,500 turned and made off at top speed for the safety of Inverness. Their arrival in such disorder so alarmed the Earl of Loudon that he made up his mind to quit Inverness itself before the vengeful hordes of Highlanders swept in from the east. The whole of his force made ready for immediate departure and did not consider they were safe from disaster until they took up new positions in Sutherlandshire, 70 miles distant.

Fraser and his five companions, pausing only to pick up the dirk of a piper who had been killed in the first volley from the muskets, returned in triumph to the Hall. He was promoted to the rank of Captain and subsequently fought with great bravery at Culloden. He is still remembered as the hero of what has come to be known as the Rout of Moy.

◆◆◆

Old stories of the Highlands still bring a chuckle. One is told of a housewife who was given a lovely large fowl. As she lived alone she realised it was too big just for her so she invited the neighbours in to share the feast. Politely she asked the guest nearest her what part she would like. "A leg, if you please," replied the neighbour. The next to be asked also opted for a leg . . . and so did the next two. The old lady regarded them all severely, and banged down the carver. "Div ye think id's a bloody spider I'm carvan?" she inquired in exasperation.

War broke out in the Haugh

MY memories are mostly centred around the Merkinch District. The bus travelling from Inverness to Kessock Ferry was an old Albion with solid wheels, because tyres hadn't come into fashion at that time. The driver was the late Mr W. Greig, who charged one penny for the fare and he packed the passengers and their "clobber" in like sardines. It was common to see boys (and I was one of them) sitting cross-legged, holding on to crates of hens, etc., bought from the late Mr Michie's sale-room.

Another form of transport I used was a steam-driven lorry from an agricultural store on Thornbush Road. The driver would slow down, where the Railway Bridge crosses the road at the back of the Clach Park, to allow the school children on and they got a lift to the back station almost every morning.

At one time soldiers were billeted at Clach Park and they were very kind to us when we went there to play and often gave us something to eat — and how we relished those tit-bits! No soup ever tasted so delicious. There were barracks too, on Telford Road which we called "The Old Militia Barracks" and, when they were no longer used, I attended the sale of all the old uniforms, etc. The late Mr Jack (Exchange) bought most of the cases of wine and one bottle of champagne was opened for tasting and I sampled it too.

Sometime about the end of the First World War there existed a state of emergency in the town. It was believed to have started in a pub in the Haugh and, in no time, it became quite out of control, so much so that it spread all over the town and the Army as well as Police were on duty to maintain law and order; and there was quite a number of casualties. On Anderson Street, the block of flats near the river later became known as "Hill Sixty", probably because it was supposed to resemble the battle of that name during the war. American sailors were thrown over the balconies of the flats and some into the river.   Eventually the culprits were rounded up and confined to the Infant Section of Merkinch School.   We youngsters were fascinated to see them being kissed through the fence by their girl-friends, as they passed on their way to work at the Tweed Mill on Telford Street.

Before the Americans left Inverness they gave a great big party and concert in the Rose Street Drill Hall and hundreds of children were presented with beautiful and expensive gifts.

Part of the Capel Inch, in these days, was taken over as a fair-ground and the shows came just after the Nairn Games.   The place would be thronged with people, at that time.

On our way to the Merkinch School, we rubbed the "lucky stone" embedded in the wall of a house on Lochalsh Road and wished a wish.   The stone is still there and well polished — so, if you pass that way, give it a rub and, who knows, your wish may be granted.

Our Schoolmaster ruled his pupils with a rod of iron.   Even at the Christmas Party or Sports Day we were like soldiers on parade. He blew his whistle for every move.   We were very glad when he left and we got a new headmaster (Mr Duncan MacKenzie) who gave us great encouragement in boths sports and education.

We had another good teacher, who wouldn't put up with any nonsense from unruly pupils in the class.   When they got out of hand (which was a common occurrence), he dealt with them in his own way.   First of all, he locked the door, took off his jacket and had a stand-up fight and, usually, the culprit ended up with a smacked bottom.

Following World War I there was the General Strike and the fuel situation became severe.   Permission was granted to cut down trees at Leachkin to ease the situation and a continual stream of people with prams and barrows, etc., could be seen wending their way, with loads of firewood to burn, to cook with and for heating.

The "gang" made fine Terriers

FROM our "gang" wars and as the years rolled by, the majority of the local lads joined the Territorials which were the Seaforth Highlanders. Had we not received good basic training in our younger days? Two evenings each week were taken up training in the local Drill Hall, then a fortnight in camp during the summer. The glowing reports of those who participated attracted more recruits for the next session. Dreghorn, Tain, Barry, Buddon, Battle Honours, The Castle Bar and the City Centre! The Territorial Army camp fortnight was perhaps the only opportunity for a change of scenery and holiday break. They arrived home bronzed and fit after a strenuous fortnight with memories of visits to various cities in the south and (whisper it) the first taste of "John Barleycorn"!

The Anti Aircraft Battery was formed in 1938 and for those who were rather conscious of their knobbly knees, this was the unit. "Yours Truly" opted for this mob. We were issued with breeches, puttees and spurs! — along with the usual kit required. Spurs! Nearest we got to a horse was when Angie McNaughton used to leave Wordie's horse and lorry outside the Territorial Hall while he went home for his dinner. The puttees had to be wound from below the kneecap to the ankle. Talk about a stick of rock! However, a few weeks of patient instruction works wonders and the P.S.I. must have been a satisfied man seeing us marching to the Railway Station en route to our first camp under the command of Col. G. D. K. Murray who, prior to the Battery's formation, was Commanding Officer of the Seaforth Territorials.

The training at camp we took in our stride. The intricacies of gun drill and "dummy runs" during the winter months proved fruitful. The real thing now! We were shown the gun park. 4.5in., 3.7in. and 3in. A.A. guns waiting to be fired! A few more lectures, we

86

were to begin firing the next day. We marched down with apprehension. The place seemed to be moving with officers and very important N.C.O.s with white bands on their hats. These people — we learned later were there to check our mistakes! However, we needn't have worried, we had the highest marks of the four batteries during that fortnight!

Now a few reminiscences of that first camp which will jog some memories. When "Robin" had the nerve to wear pyjamas in our tent (had not the Quartermaster issued us with shirts which also served the purpose of nightgowns. They were large enough, anyway!). Poor Robin was thrown out of the tent until he attired himself like the rest of us! The lad (un-named) who was invited to take part in a game of cards. "How about Pontoon 'e night?" He answered "I might do. How far away is it? Is it larger than Whithorn?" His geography must have been sadly neglected!

The local lad who was on sentry-go, in the gun park, who challenged the Orderly Officer — not in the manner as laid down — "Halt! Who goes there?" but a volley of expletives which halted the Orderly Officer much more quickly! The mounting of the guard — very regimental. The military band playing "For he is a handsome Territorial!" We'd take stock of ourselves and it was difficult not to smile! There was a great spirit among these lads and we can look back to the friendships and camaraderie which began before the "ball burst".

During 1939, we had to do a month's training and were only a fortnight home when we received our mobilisation orders. Our first parade was at the Drill Hall to be issued with five pounds mobilisation money. We then had to load our equipment on lorries which were driven to Scrabster then on to a ship to be taken to our "war station" in Orkney. Our second parade (!) was dodging into the nearby licensed premises during the loading of the lorries. Eventually we were organised and left Scrabster with mixed feelings ready to do our bit. A far cry from the game of "gang-warfare" of our young days.

Time was more elastic, then

WHEN I was young, time seemed a much more elastic commodity than it is today and no-one seemed to rush around, asking everyone else every five minutes "What's the time?"

Our day was governed by the School Bell (THE BELL, THE BELL, THE **B E L L**), the Railway and the Foundry "Hooters" (as we called them) and, in the evening we knew the Cathedral Bells pealed at six o'clock and the "Town Bells" at eight o'clock and ten o'clock.

The "Eight o'clock Bells" reminded us that time was getting on and it would soon be time to go indoors for the night. If we were still out by "Ten o'clock Bells" we would get into hot water at home . . . if not from the policeman who patrolled our beat. Sometimes, when coming home after spending an evening playing "Ludo" or knitting in a friend's house a stone's throw from my own, I would be terrified lest I should come across P.C. L------'s fat, rosy, smiling form — because his appearance belied his annoyance and he would tell us, in no uncertain terms, what he thought of children who stayed out late at night! All the same, I don't think the Inverness streets held so many dangers for youngsters as they do today.

However, it is not of the Six, Eight or Ten o'clock Bells I am writing but of a story I was told by my blind cousin recently. Peggy is around seventy and has a fund of tales of childhood memories of Inverness. One of her tales is the story of the "Nine o'clock Bells" which set all the people in the town agog with consternation and excitement.

According to Peggy, this event happened away back in 1912, and she was one of the "participants" in the affair. Peggy is an expert pianist and singer and is immensely fond of music. One evening, she and some other musical friends from the Blind School accompanied one of their schoolmates to the Church where he

88

played the organ on Sundays and where he was allowed to practise whenever he wanted.

All went well and they probably had a grand time singing and listening to the organ, when someone said that it was time to go home. When they reached the outside door they found, to their horror, that they had been accidentally locked in, probably by the beadle, who perhaps did not know of their presence or had supposed that they had already gone away.

The children all went around the Church, trying the doors and windows to see if they could open them and they had just decided that they would have to spend the night where they were, when one bright person suggested that someone should try to reach the belfry and raise the alarm by ringing the bells.

Once it was agreed who would perform this dangerous mission, the rest helped in locating where the belfry was and then helped in hoisting the brave fellow through the hatch. After a breath-taking ten minutes or so, they all heaved a sigh of relief when they heard the great bell pealing at around nine o'clock. I have no idea what sort of a peal it was — and whether it was just one loud clang or a clatter of cacophony but, anyway, it threw the townspeople into confusion; and it was a surprised bellringer who discovered the culprits, who had dared to ring "Ten o'clock Bells" at nine o'clock!

As a sequel to this escapade, Peggy told me that, after it happened, she (and some of her school friends) were secretly allowed to climb up to the belfry, guided by the youthful bell-ringer, so that they could catch his spirit of adventure. It's a wonder to me that no-one was hurt. On the contrary, Peggy just said, "We thought it was a great laugh!"

How do you kill a clock?

AN Aberdeen chemist took over business in Thurso just after the Second World War. He had great difficulty in understanding the local dialect as the following story shows. One day an elderly lady asked him for a good strong "Redder"; another local enlightened him that the lady wanted a large comb. Shortly afterwards a customer asked for "Something for killing clocks." He was stumped again until he was told that "clocks" were beetles, cockroaches, etc!

The driver who transported the German P.O.W.s who were interned in Watten Prison Camp told me this story: many P.O.W.s were used on the farms. This particular farmer was noted for his meanness. At break-time he gave the group a pail of water and two loaves! The driver told me he never saw potatoes planted the way these Germans did after that affront. In groups of three — one "dimpled", the second put down the potato and the third used his heel and crushed each potato! I couldn't tell you what kind of crop that farmer got out of his Kerrs Pinks!

During the early days of the motor car people from North Sutherland made very infrequent visits to the Town — perhaps 3-6 months, sometimes longer. This story concerns one of these people. He called at a local drapers and said he'd come to pay a small account. Searching through his books this draper could find nothing, but the customer insisted that he owed him 3s6d for a certain article and said the draper must accept the money as he never owed anybody anything and always paid his bills. As he was leaving, he stopped suddenly and said to the draper "By the way, that is a fine suit you've hanging there I would have bought it, the price is so reasonable, but I'm afraid I haven't taken enough money down with me. Do you think you could let me have it and I shall pay it when I come down next time?" The draper, impressed with the man's honesty, let him have it. He got the suit for the 3s6d which he hadn't owed the draper in the first instance and was never seen around again!

Superstition seems to have died out. Thurso, like all other fishing ports, was rife with superstition. I shall recount some of the stories I have heard down by the harbour.

One young lad called on a boat crew when they were sharing out their takings in the galley. He asked them for scraps of bread. "What for?", asked one. "For my rabbits", replied the lad. He was surprised when the men swore at him and chased him off the boat. There is an electronics engineer who came from England and set up business in Thurso and repaired the echo-sounders and R.T. sets of the fishing boats. On this occasion, he was to go out with the crew and test the equipment in the bay. He had made arrangements to see them at a certain time but had been delayed at the salmon bothy at Forss. When he arrived at the harbour the crew were waiting and he apologised for the delay saying that he'd been to the salmon bothy. The crew refused point blank and the engineer went away wondering what he had done to offend them — as did the lad who wanted scraps for his rabbit. These two words are taboo and considered to be bad luck.

During the days of the small fishing boats, perhaps three or four of a crew, one fisherman couldn't find his "bonnet" so he put on his bowler. His boat returned with the largest catch. The following day, **all** the crews wore their bowler hats!

Should you be heard whistling, the fishermen chased us. They interpreted that as "blowing for wind" and there would be a gale springing up.

Should the fishermen happen to meet either of two certain old ladies they would not go to sea that day as they were considered to be very unlucky.

During the days when they baited hand-lines, nothing was done until midnight on Sunday. Any other evening everything would be prepared for the next day's fishing by nine o'clock.

Then there was the ceremony of "burning the witch". Perhaps they would get rid of a member of the crew who was considered to be to blame for small catches. His bunk bed was taken out to sea and set on fire. I remember an elderly chap telling me that he and a friend rowed their boat quite a distance thinking it was a boat on fire only to find that some crew had been "burning the witch".

As children we used to tip-toe past a house where a death had occurred.

We would not stand on a snail as it would bring rain!

Spill salt, we had to throw a pinch over the left shoulder.

"Don't makes faces, or should the wind change you'll be left like that."

Should we find a dead animal or bird we would spit on the carcase while passing. Then one wouldn't pick up a disease!

Nose-bleeds: One got the biggest key in the house and it was placed on the back of the neck. I realise now it was only to keep one's head back until the blood had congealed.

Eggshells or fish-bones were never thrown on to the fire as it was considered unlucky!

◆◆◆

The invariable custom in many parts of the Highlands after a death used to be for invitations to be issued for the funeral. One crofter's wife in Lochaber, displeased because her husband had not been invited to a certain funeral, remarked peevishly: "Whait, you. We'll have a funeral of our own and **they** won't get an invitation!"

Fairies are
only human!

THERE ARE still plenty of people in the Highlands, even in these days of industrialisation and sophistication, who are not too ready to discount tales of fairies, elves and goblins. Traditions die hard, and the traditions of Britain's wildest and most mysterious region are firmly rooted in superstition.

Not all that long ago, fairies were very real indeed to the Highlanders. What is more, they were considered to have strong and definite associations with humans and to share a good many human weaknesses and frailties. Passions, for instance.

It was once strongly held that fairies were amorous creatures who were by no means averse to human attachments. Indeed, many were considered to seek out mortals expressly to engage in illicit relationships. Incredible as it may seem today, many Highlanders believed that not a few fairies found themselves pregnant in consequence. There is an oft-told story about this in the Cairngorm region.

In that area, so the tale goes, there lived a midwife with an extensive practice. Indeed, she was, by all accounts, the best midwife in the Highlands. One night she was preparing for bed when there came a loud and urgent knocking on the door. This was not an uncommon occurrence for a midwife, and as she went to the door she was already prepared for a night excursion to a croft or a cottage.

When she opened the door she saw a rider and horse, both panting from their haste. The rider entreated the midwife to jump on the horse behind him instantly, saying that a good woman's life was in danger. When the midwife asked for time to change her clothes and prepare for the journey, the rider agitatedly refused and begged her to come just as she was. Seeing that he was in such distress, she gave in, and off they went at full gallop.

As they sped through the night, she asked the rider where they were going and how far they would have to travel. The only reply she could get was that she would be well paid for her trouble. This did not satisfy the midwife, who began to get alarmed as the road became rougher and more and more remote. She plied the rider with questions and was plainly so distressed that he feared she would be in no fit state to carry out her duties when they arrived. So he decided to make a clean breast of it.

"Do not be alarmed, madam," he said, "but prepare yourself for a surprise. I am taking you to a fairy habitation where there is a fairy lady in distress. Take no distress, I beseech you. I promise that you will be unharmed and will, in due course, be returned safely to your dwelling well recompensed."

This was spoken in such sincerity that the midwife lost her fears and resigned herslf to whatever might happen. When they reached the end of the journey the midwife found the fairy lady in anything but easy circumstances, but her skill and ability overcame all difficulties and eventually the fairy gave birth to a fine boy. Much joy and rejoicing followed and the midwife was offered any gift she cared to choose. The midwife thought hard and long, and eventually made up her mind.

"I ask that whomsoever I, or my heirs, should attend in a professional capacity, should be assured of a safe and speedy delivery," she said. The favour was instantly conferred upon her and, so the story goes, passed on to her daughters and granddaughters.

Well, it is a curious story for those of us who were brought up to think of fairies as remote, innocent, spirit creatures, but many districts in the Highlands can tell of something similar. Indeed, not far away from the midwife in our tale, was the renowned shoemaker of Tomintoul. Just over 100 years ago he was confessing, in his old age, to dalliances with a fairy as a young man.

Apparently the old man's confessions were received not with an indulgent nod — but with general expressions of wonder. And respect.

Fairies were one thing, but water-kelpies were another. Very much another. They were infernal agents in the pay of Satan and were extremely versatile in an amphibious way. They were reputed to live in lochs and pools bordering public roads and to be capable of taking many forms. Their principal task was to destroy human beings without giving them time to prepare for the hereafter. Thus their souls would go to Satan and their bodies to the kelpie. There was one restraint, however. The kelpie was not allowed to touch a human being of his own accord unless the human acted first. The kelpie therefore appeared in the form most likely to attract a human, the favourite disguise being a fine horse richly and expensively accoutered.

Well, there is a story about a kelpie who lived in and around Loch Ness. He, too, had the appearance of a fine riding steed, so it was small wonder that when a certain Mr James Macgregor caught sight of him on his way to Inverness, his attention was instantly caught. What the kelpie did not know, however, that Mr Macgregor had long hoped and prayed for the chance to meet the Loch Ness kelpie and to punish him for all the atrocities he had committed.

No sooner did Macgregor spy the fine horse browsing at the roadside than he recognised it as the infamous kelpie in disguise. He dismounted, walked up to the horse, drew his sword and administered a tremendous blow on its nose, breaking the jaw and cutting the bridle allowing the bit to fall to the ground. As the horse struggled to its feet, Macgregor pocketed the bit and awaited the bitter conflict which seemed inevitable. But to his amazement the kelpie began to reproach him for acting so cruelly.

"Why have you treated me thus" he asked. "I have heard of you as a man of honour and humanity. What honour is there in such a savage attack on a poor defenceless animal like me — horse, or kelpie — when I did you no harm? I should be perfectly justified in returning your assault twofold, but that is not my desire. If you will return the bit which you have pocketed I shall leave you in peace."

Macgregor responded by telling the kelpie just what he thought of him and flatly refusing to pass over the bit. The kelpie said he was not surprised to know that Macgregor had a poor opinion of him. "We kelpies," he said, "have to engage in many disagreeable undertakings because we have no choice in the matter. All I want now is my bit and an end to this confrontation."

Macgregor sensed that the bit had special significance, so he decided to play a waiting game. "I have not changed my opinion of kelpies in general," he said, "although I must confess that I am a little more disposed to you now that I have heard you speak. Certainly you may have your bit, but first tell me what makes it so special."

The kelpie was delighted. The bridle, he said, was issued to kelpies to enable them to transform and transport themselves at will. Without it their power was at an end . . . and death would follow within 24 hours. "I must confess that if you had not severed my bridle with your blow I should have broken every bone in your body. Now that you have my bit, you are stronger than I. Furthermore it gives you some of the powers of a kelpie. Look through it and you will see fairies, witches and devils all flying around you."

Needless to say, Macgregor was astonished by all this. But he was not disarmed by the kelpie's demeanour. "Thank you very much for the information," he said, "but I could not now bear to part with the bit. I bid you good day." And off he went on his road home.

Such ingratitude appalled the kelpie. He begged and pleaded, but Macgregor was adamant. He threatened, but Macgregor flourished his sword and the kelpie fell back cowed. When the house came in sight, the kelpie galloped ahead vowing that Macgregor would never enter. The imperturbable Macgregor was not concerned. Going to the back window, he threw the bit to his wife who was in the kitchen. Then he went back to the kelpie.

"You are a pretty poor negotiator," he said. "I now do not have the bit, and there is no way you can get it."

The kelpie snarled. "We shall see about that," he said, and turned to bound into the house.

"Just a minute," said Macgregor. "Haven't you forgotten something?" He pointed to the lintel over the door.

The kelpie looked upward . . . and cringed. For there on the wall was a rowan cross: death to all evil spirits which passed beneath.

The kelpie slunk off, defeated and in the knowledge that he had only a few more hours to live.

And, believe it or not, you can still see rowan crosses on some dwellings in the Highlands. You never know . . .

Market labourers at Inverness worked hard and long for little money when the group in this picture was photographed. The picture was probably taken in the 1860's.

This roadside smithy — the Victorian counterpart of the service station — was at Bunchrew. It was definitely "service while you wait!"

Errand boy got 5s.
— and earned it!

IN BYGONE days most goods arrived at Thurso on Thursdays
by cargo-steamer; thence by lorry to the various shops. Everything
was in bulk — sugar in 2cwt. bags, flour in boll bags — even bird-
seed arrived in $\frac{1}{2}$ cwts.! These goods were ordered from wholesale
firms based in Aberdeen, Leith and Edinburgh. Commercial
travellers called monthly to collect orders. Their visits were welcomed — they always had a wealth of new stories and tricks (remember Peter Angus of J. & J. Tod, Leith?). Peter never failed to
have some new trick "up his sleeve". He even had a cuckoo-
sounding two-tone horn attached to his motor car! J. Starkey —
a famed heavyweight games champion in his young days — was a
whisky representative. How I used to marvel at his strength in
cracking walnuts between two fingers. (It took me all my time to
crack a peanut!).

As an errand boy in a grocery shop one had to work very hard.
Should one work on Saturday only, the wage was the princely sum
of 2/-! Full-time errand boys received from 5/- to 7/6 per week
(wages varied from shop to shop). The routine was much the same
every day. In the morning, the first task was to sweep the pavement
in front of the premises, then wash the windows. A half-barrel of
salt herring was then trundled to the door (the slops of herring brine
splashing on stockings as one struggled to place the barrel). A metal
stand was then placed outside, vegetables were displayed on the
lower shelves and a few salted dried fish placed on the top shelf.
The smell of herring "bree" and salt fish lingering in the nostrils!
Then to polish the brasses (including the brass weights ranging from
$\frac{1}{4}$ ounce to 7lb. Luckily the heavier weights were made of cast
iron!). Chop firewood, fetch coal — the jobs were never-ending.
"Fetch this!" "Fetch that!" "Run here!" "Run there!" (what
would the shop assistants do without the poor errand boy?) He

seemed to be at everyone's beck and call! You would perhaps hear a customer ask for salt herring, you try to creep away unobserved, to dodge the inevitable — "Get a newspaper and gie 'e wifie a half-a-dizzen herrin' " — or "Fill a half-a-ston' o' tatties." Have you ever had the revolting experience of "raikan" in a bag of potatoes and your searching hand closing on a mushy, rotten potato? Ugh!

Some grocery shops supplied paraffin — another "foosum" job! Ah, well this is the bottom of the ladder. Perhaps, some day we may become managers or have a shop of our own, then it will be our turn to order some poor laddie around. Errand boys were "raikan oot" ashes and setting fires. The majority of shops did not close until 8 p.m. on Saturday nights. "Id's cheinged days!"

If the shop had a "van trade" — retailing groceries around the rural districts — all the goods had to be made ready in small packages. Cheese and butter arrived in 56lb. lots, these had to be cut and weighed. Sugar, cereals, etc., had to be "bagged" and tied with string. The assistants did the bulk of that work but the errand boy was always there to lend a hand. I wonder why we didn't develop large muscular shoulders with the large baskets we had to carry on our arms!

We looked forward to Christmas and New Year. Although we received an odd twopence or threepence on our regular deliveries throughout the year, we were sure of a tidy sum during the festive season. We would receive sums ranging from 1s to 10s — a fortune! I remember one customer to whom I delivered messages every week during the whole year, gave me sixpence for my Christmas Box (whisper it!) I wasn't too careful with that person's eggs in the next few weeks' deliveries.

As you will realise, our jobs were many and varied — plus "obligements" we had to do for some customers. I remember one day, a customer arrived with two live hens — would we kill them and deliver to her home? Yes! Certainly! I was told: "Take 'at hens till 'e store and thraa thur necks." I meekly carried the hens to the store, ten minutes later one of the shop assistants came in wondering about the hold-up. The hens were still alive. I didn't have the heart to kill them. "Show them here." The assistant grabbed one with a flourish. "Aal show ye" — placed the hen under his left "oxter" and pulled the neck with his right hand. The head of the hen came away in his hand. He dropped the headless hen in astonishment — the hen took a half dozen steps and collapsed. The other hen — he bent the neck over and held it until it choked. I must admit I never learned the intricacies of "thraa-ing" necks, but I got a "tanner" tip from the wifie.

The day's work began at 5 a.m.

I HAVE several recollections of a crofter's life years ago. The wife had to be an early riser. Five o'clock saw her up and making a cup of tea for husband and bairns before going out to the byre to milk two cows at least. The milk had to be sieved into tin basins and left to set. The cream that formed on top was removed next day with a skimmer and put into a large earthenware jar. Butter muslin was tied over it to keep out flies and dust.

When the jar was full, the cream was poured into a churn to be made into butter. This was quite a lengthy job as the churn had to be scrupulously clean and scalded before pouring in the cream. The churn was barrel-shaped and placed on a stand. By turning a handle it went over and over and by using one's judgement you knew when the butter had "come". It had to be washed in cold water before being clapped by wooden clappers to extract all the butter milk. Lumps were weighed and then formed into one pound and half pound pats, the top being decorated usually with the clappers.

An older sister and I visited the crofter's wife one day; to get to her house we had to walk down a cart track. She saw us coming and told us when we got there that she had hidden the churn as she thought we were tinkers. There was an old belief that the butter wouldn't "come" if tinkers came to her door.

Her kitchen floor was of clay and I recall an incident when her husband's nose bled he let the blood drop on the floor and then said "Wipe that up, woman," and she did. The fireplace was a large open one with a swee. She had a three-legged pot that she used to boil potatoes in for dinner. Potatoes, meal and herring were the main stand-bys.

A large ashet was placed in the centre of the table and her usual comment was "Tatties out and tatties in" as potatoes scattered on to the table and floor when she turned the huge pot upside down. Red herrings were served with the tatties.

Dinner over, the Book was brought down from a recess in the wall beside the horse hair sofa. A chapter was read, a psalm sung, and a prayer made before the day's work was resumed. The dog, named Fly, always joined in the singing. I loved to hear her do this. Some afternoons the crofter's wife brought in a pot of tar. She put it on the swee, swung it on to the fire to thin down, then, with a long-handled brush, she applied it to the jambs. The brilliance of that shine never failed to fascinate me.

Marketing her surplus butter, crowdie and eggs wasn't any easy job. She dressed in her best shawl and bonnet and set off with her wares in a large wicker basket with a handle over the top. She had to walk a couple of miles to a ferry where the ferryman rowed her across to the nearest town. The money she got for her goods provided for some of the essentials in life; and we talk of the "Good Old Days!"

Surprise! She wanted pay!

TWO OLD stories come to mind. Lexie drew her O.A.P. and had it supplemented by the Laird who owned the estate on which she lived. She also had a rent-free house.

For these concessions she was asked to do light jobs on the estate. At first she was delighted to do them; but, after a while she felt she ought to get a pay packet at the end of the month like other employees.

A daily job in the "season" time was to rake the gravel smooth on either side of the drive leading to the Castle. When a few weeks went by and there was no sight of Lexie, the lady from the Castle called to ask if she was well.

"Yes, my lady, I'm quite well," she said, "but I didn't get paid for the work I did."

"Oh, I thought you would work for the pleasure of it," the lady said.

"Work is no more a pleasure to me than it is to anybody else," retorted Lexie.

How old Rory, the shepherd, could forecast the weather so accurately never ceased to amaze me. "Fine day, Rory," I remarked on a remarkably mild sunny one in January. "Oh, lassie," he replied, "this is a ghost of a day. Can't you see the low-lying clouds running after one another?" I watched, and they were. His prediction was "We will get a storm before the week is out." We did!

He was a dab hand at putting a taste on a story and when his opening remark was "Well, I mind" I knew I was in luck for one of Rory's reminiscences. He would sometimes drop in for a cup; and once I got what one might call a left-handed compliment from him; "That's a good scone" he said "The farmhouse fresh butter can make it feel that way," I said. "Oh, maybe that's what it is," was Rory's nonchalant reply.

101

2s. 6d. clothed
four children

I REMEMBER a big shop in Union Street, Inverness — The Home and Colonial. They were experts on clapping your butter into a nice square and shaping it into exact measures. It was a marvel to watch. Then there was Santa Claus' Cave where the lovely soft music beckoned you to a fairyland. Both shops were in Union Street — one where a draper's shop is and Santa's Cave was where Arnotts is now.

Coming to the Market; on the 28th of each month all the country workers changed each other's bosses. The sheep and cows were driven through the street and the farm workers' wives put out their wares of ginger men, sugar mice and lovely yellow puff candy. The Nairn fish wives sold lovely juicy speldings and cockles at 1d a bowl. Also in Union Street we loved to see Dr Bodie doing his trance feats at the Music Hall. Coming now to High Street, Woolworths was a great event in Inverness. All goods were 6d. I dressed my four children from head to foot and it cost 2/6d. Gramophone records were 6d each.

Now to Church Street to watch the beautiful ladies and gentlemen with their lovely dresses and kilts attending the Northern Meeting Ball. We watched them into the early hours of the morning. The Caledonian Hotel was very busy. In summer the great trip was a day across the ferry.

We had street entertainment such as the German Band and an Irish Paddy singing and dancing. We had a lovely band and pierrots You could get a chair to sit on and enjoy all the entertainment for a penny.

I remember the suspension bridge. It took you up to Bridge Street and the first shop you saw was a Mr Melville's shoe and boot shop and the lovely Tacketie boots on show were a joy to look upon as they were to be our "Xmas Stocking."   Boys and girls wore these boots.

I remember the gallant soldiers billeted in the schools and in Margaret Street Drill Hall which is now Cameron Hall.   Invalid soldiers recovering from their wounds took up their duties guarding Inverness Station and other parts.   When I became old enough I decided to do something for my country.   I went to have an interview with the Station Master and became a Porteress.   We saw many trains of German prisoners of war and they really showed us how they hated us.   So we saw the soldiers come through the station to begin their guard duty and so it was I fell in love with one of these soldiers and married him in August, 1918.

Div ye forget
yur mither towng?

THERE is a quotation which is often used: "Never forget yur mither towng," which means more than one's manner of speech. It also means do not be ashamed of your place of birth. Do not forget your friends if you should have climbed a few steps higher on the social ladder. In short — no snobbery!

May I continue with a list of "Thirsa wordies" which come to mind:— Antle, Argue; Aafil, Awful; Alviz, Always; Blost, to Boast; Blooter, Heavy Shower; Bowg, Stomach; Bools, Boulders; Cheeg, Jerk; Chiel, Chap; Cowped, Overturned; Cownan, Crying; Clootie, Cloth; Div Ye, Do You; Dirl, Vibrate; Dowpag, Cigarette End; Dunder Heid, Stupid Person; Foosome, Filthy; Firnent, In Front Of; Feil, Mentally Deficient; Glounk, Gulp; Gushlan, To Work in a Messy Way; Gluff, Fright; Gutters, Mud; Heishle, Untidy Collection; Hirplan, Limping; Ivenow or Ivanow, Just Now.

The letter "J" is unknown! e.g., Cham, Jam; Chames, James; Chelly, Jelly; Chon, John, etc.; Ken, Know; Kinch, Jerk or Twist; Loogard, Slap on Ear; Loogs, Ears; Loon, Boy; Lowe, Flame; Lum, Chimney; Maw, Seagull; Nev, Fist; Preeg, Plead; Peedie, Small; Peetie, Pity; Pech, Pant; Peedlan or Trowan, Dodging Classes; Quait, Quiet; Rillens, Anything worn to ribbons; Reet or Rake, To turn things over untidily; Skowth, Scopt; Spounks, Matches; Stroosh, Quick Swagger; Smyagger, Smear; Skint, Splash; Skutch, Dash Around; Shochad, Lapwing; Sneck, Snib; Skirlan, Screaming; Sprowgie, Sparrow; Stoor, Dust; Scrayed, Dried; Trock, Rubbish; Trauchled, Exhausted; Wheest, Be Quiet; Wraxed, Stretched.

Perhaps some of our older readers will remember the "brat". It was a coarse apron made from a sugar bag and used for rough work — (pre-washing machine days). Where could one have a more expressive word than "Rivven" which means Torn Apart.

104

I must finish with a story of a local who was trying to sell a second-hand radio. In trying to convince the prospective buyer, he told him: "She's a good set and has never been 'wraxed'. She's never been used for foreign stations!"

❧❧❧

In the Great War booms and nets supported by huge logs protected the entrance to the Cromarty Firth. No fishing was allowed in the Firth at night and no ships at all were allowed to be under way. The Americans had two big depot ships moored at Kessock.

Apart from wartime, there used to be 50 to 60 sailing boats fishing with drift nets out of Avoch. All fishing was done by chance — and plenty were caught. Motor vessels have badly affected the fishing and, of course, we now have the "benefit" of echo meters.

My finger-
powered disco!

As a child I had wonderful parents who shared in all my fun. My first memory at Cannich was my "housie" which I made in a shed. Oh, what a great place: cups, dishes, lino on the floor, but best of all a gramophone with records. It didn't matter the gramophone would not work! We spent hours spinning the records round and round with our fingers until we could just make out the tune.

I shall never forget my mother's cooking, especially her pans of broth so thick with fresh vegetables that you could hardly get your spoon in it. The smell of roasting rabbit was just lovely, and how I loved the thick gravy she always managed to make. *And* the scones and oatcakes that used to melt in my mouth, runny with butter and, sometimes, syrup. Her jam boiling on the open fire in a big, black pan made my mouth water . . . and never to be forgotten were the clootie dumplings. Oh for some of those today!

Dad had a great "pulley" — his wire ropes across the river. To this he would fasten a seat. Once installed, you could pull yourself across. There was great pride — and some showing-off — when one had actually accomplished the crossing. Very often in summer we would go to "Primrose Isle", a lovely place with miles of lovely primroses growing wild. We picked great bunches of them to take home, and to this day I can still smell that beautiful "Primrose Isle."

Expeditions to Inverness were a great treat, and often I would be taken to the pictures. The fare, as I recall, was 2s 6d. It is over £1 now! The night before the trip, hair was washed and we bathed in a big tin bath before a log fire. Our clothes for the journey were all laid out, and we children were always awake long before our parents got up.

Tramps and pedlars

TRAMPS and pedlars were familiar, colourful sights in days gone by. I remember a one-eyed Irishman named Paddy Gaynor who was always ready for a fight. His companion on the pedlar's box was a monkey, but during an altercation in the taproom the monkey was killed. A local stalwart in Lochaber, Big Hugh, was accused of the deed . . . but it was a brave man who, long after, would ask in Hugh's company "Who killed Paddy's monkey?" Hugh did not take kindly to such innuendos.

The local general merchant stocked all the odds and ends for pedlars at wholesale prices, and was never once let down in payment. Honesty was always the pedlars' policy at least as far as he was concerned.

There was one named Willie Jamieson who had a strange physical disability: his teeth never grew. He was admired by all his acquaintances as one who could make a jingling rhyme on any subject you chose. He kept all his belongings on a small wheelbarrow. One day, in pouring rain, I met him on the road and asked where he was bound. "Och, just a wee daunder as far as Lochailort," he said. That was 25 miles away! He was well liked by all the calachs, who made sure he got a piece and tea. He had to repay them with a packet of pins, or something of that sort. Sad, indeed, was Willie's end. He pitched his tent near a sand-pit. The pit caved in and he was smothered.

Tommy Adams, an Englishman, failed on account of eyesight, to become an engineer. He took to the road with pony and trap and was consequently a posh kind of pedlar. One day he tethered his pony to a canal house fence. The pony broke the railing and plunged, cart and all, into the canal basin. It took a whole squad of lock keepers to fish the outfit out. .

Another wandering Willie was "The Bully", so called beacuse he was somewhat handy — and ready — with his fists. He and another tramp, Scotty Parker, fell foul of one another and the ensuing fight resulted in "The Bully" being knocked through a plate glass window. The local Bobby marched them both off to gaol.

"Lord Dundonald," an Islander, wore as many coats as skins on an onion. His favourite dosshouse was behind the distillery. One night when he could not get to the distillery he chose to sleep in an outhouse near the sea. He was found frozen stiff the next morning.

Strange people, those "Kings of the road." Now they have all gone.

Haircut lasted all summer!

WHEN I was a lad at school all jotters and exercise books had to be paid for by our parents and I assure you they did not last long! Woe betide you, should your sums be incorrect — two strokes of the teacher's pencil, damaging a few more pages in the process. The jotter disintegrating into single pages, as it was "hurled" back with these words ringing in your ears — "peesh posh", "tommy rot". This was one of our favourite teachers of the "old school" and she had a heart of gold.

On Fridays we would be on our best behaviour, as on that day she chose two boys to carry the girls' sewing bags to her home for which we were rewarded with a sixpence each. So you can imagine the amount of angels in that classroom on a Friday!

"Half-penny worth of hard bread". Yes! We looked for bargains as soon as we started school! We'd get two cakes of the previous day's baking, from the nearby bakery. There would be a queue of children, and when one arrived at the counter it was pandemonium; some trying to get in, others pushing to get out. The morning break did not last long, just enough time to swallow two dry "bunnies" and a dash to the "pump" for a drink of water — no free milk in these days! These teachers had a difficult job, moulding us into useful citizens and must have looked back with pride when they heard of the achievements of some "Thirsa boyagies" who are now scattered all over the world.

How often we would make a mistake in our jotters then discover we had no rubber. A cautious look round hoping teacher wasn't seeing you then wet the tip of the finger and rub out the error. Teacher sees you and besides giving you a telling-off, you get a "loogard" (that one has got you beat!) to remind you to use a rubber next time.

The "tawse" or strap was in regular use. We used to rub our hands with resin (a tip handed down from the older boys). This was supposed to take the sting out of the smack. I don't know, but I am sure this all depended on how hard the teacher used the strap! "Hand out!" We invariably drew our hand back, making teacher miss, much to the glee of our classmates. The strap would continue on its downward stroke towards the teacher's legs. Luckily they didn't wear mini-skirts or teacher's legs would have suffered more than our hands. The teacher always won and we'd walk back to our seats with a forced grin and tears in our eyes.

One teacher must have disliked our broad "Thirsa" dialect. I remember during a reading lesson, the word "bird" was in the passage. Of course we pronounced it "burd" so he went through the whole class until one bright spark satisfied him with the pronunciation "berd". We all looked on that as a "cissy" way of saying it and I think he gave up all hope of converting us! Talking of pronunciation, I used to attend the Salvation Army Sunday School and the English officer taught us a new chorus. Her accent had me baffled! The beginning of the verse was "Running over". I joined in the singing with the rest but my interpretation was "Ranny Nova"!

When I look around at the present-day hair styles I think of the times when we would be sent to the barber with threepence for a "pole" — a close cropped haircut — leaving a "dossan" — a tuft of hair in the front. This lasted us through the summer holidays; we would then revert back to the orthodox "short back and sides".

"Checky Forbas", the attendance officer or "whipper-in" as he was commonly called, had his hands full. How many Thurso readers left home for school, bag on back, shouting cheerio to his ever-trusting mum then when out of sight of home, made a detour to the Mall? Previous to the building of the boating and paddling ponds there were small streams on that side of the river. Perhaps we'd look for "brandles" or small eels then a bit of horseplay finishing with attempts to "jump-'e-streamie". More often than not we got soaked in the process by making the width of the stream in two jumps!

We'd wend our way home collecting our schoolbags on the way and arrive home with innocent faces trying to walk silently which was very difficult, as with every step there sounded a "squelch" from our soaked shoes. Should we do this two days running Mr Forbes would be at the door then we had to face the music and leathering into the bargain when we got back to school.

110

I wonder if the boys in other classes were as unruly as us? We were to be taught the game of hockey. We weren't interested in that — "'ats a lassagies' game" were the words repeated more than once. However, orders are orders. We were marched to the "Dammies" armed with hockey sticks. At that time the Town Council would rent the field for the grazing of sheep, so, before our course of instruction we had to clear the field. The first fifteen minutes were boring and uninteresting, until one enterprising lad began using sheep droppings in place of the ball. Soon we all joined in — this was more fun — and our instructor performed some kind of dance, blowing her whistle and shouting alternately.

I must say that is the only course of instruction our class received on hockey!

Sunday
at Cilliechriost

MANY ARE the desperate and ferocious records of clan battles in the Highlands; few are so terrible as the Raid of Cilliechriost which stains the history of Ross-shire.

Many years ago there was a chapel at Cilliechriost. The building has long since crumbled and decayed, but the fearful story linked with it is still told and re-told. It all centred on the many quarrels which arose between two chiefs: Mackenzie of Kintail and Macdonnell of Glengarry. On this particular occasion there was a dispute over land and, as usual, it was not allowed to die down for lack of action. Taking advantage of the absence of the chief of the Mackenzies, the Macdonnells moved into Mackenzie country and committed great devastation under the leadership of Glengarry's son, Angus. From Kintail and Lochalsh the clan Mackenzie gathered quickly but not quickly enough to prevent Macdonnell escaping by sea with his boats laden with booty. Some of the Mackenzies ran to Eilean-donan while others sped to the narrow strait at Kyle through which the Macdonnells would have to sail.

At Eilean-donan they were furnished with two boats, arrows and ammunition. Rowing towards Kyleakin they lay in wait. They allowed the first of the Glengarry boats to pass unchallenged but the second was violently attacked. The heavily-laden boat overturned, throwing all the occupants into the sea. Many were killed as they tried to swim to safety. Those who did manage to reach the shore were despatched without mercy. Among the dead was the son Angus.

Time passed but it was not allowed to dim the memory of the defeat. Vengeance was seething in every heart and although, by then, the clan chief was an infant who could not take direct action, there was a cousin who held the office of clan captain. He could most certainly take action. And he did.

112

He was Macranuil of Lundi and he was a man of great courage and intense ferocity. Many times he had led incursions into Mackenzie territory to devastate and terrorise the countryside, but these were mere preludes for what he believed would be the culmination of his career of warfare. For this dedicated act of revenge he planned and plotted with great care. With complete disregard for his safety he disguised himself as a mendicant and wandered abroad in Mackenzie country to study the locations; to devise the best means of attack; and to plan a foray that would wash away the record of the death of his kinsmen at Kyleakin.

Such a foray would have to be of a nature that would never be forgotten. In due time he completed his reconnaissance and returned home to make his plan. It was simple in conception and horrific in execution.

In the company of the most desperate and ruthless of his clan, he made a forced march across the hills and arrived at the Chapel of Cilliechriost on a Sunday morning when it was filled with worshippers of the Mackenzie clan. As the songs of praise rang out in the morning air, he surrounded the chapel with his band of desperadoes and set fire to the thatched roof. A breeze quickly fanned the flames and a wave of horror swept through the congregation. They turned to rush to the doors and windows, only to be met by a double row of gleaming swords.

Shrieks of despair from women and children mingled with the hoarse shouts of the men. These, added to the roar and crackle of the flames, appalled even the Macdonnells — but not their captain. "Thrust them back in the flames," he shouted. "He that permits one to escape shall forever be branded as a traitor to his clan." So all were thrust back, or were cut down in the narrow porch until the dead bodies piled up to present an unsurmountable barrier to those still struggling to escape.

Hysterical mothers threw children through the windows in the last hope that the Macdonnells would spare the lives of infants. It was not to be. They were impaled on the points of the broadswords. It was a terrible sight seen only by terrible and merciless men. And during all this horror, the piper of the clan marched around the blazing chapel playing to drown the screams and to stimulate his clansmen to unflinching determination.

The flaming roof fell in on the hapless victims and stifled the few, faint cries of the last to perish. A great pall of black smoke ascended to the skies. The agonies of the Sunday morning worshippers were over. The sound of the pipes was stilled. All was quiet,

113

but the stench of death was in the air. Then to the captain of the clan and to his followers came the realisation of what they had done. Looking around them it seemed that the parish had been cleared of every living thing. In less than an hour they had sent every man, woman and child to a single, dreadful grave. Dismay and terror came to them and they turned to fly. They split into two parties, the better to make their escape. One party went by way of Urquhart; the other by Inverness. But there was to be no escape

As soon as the massacre was discovered, the Mackenzies went into action. Two bands of clansmen set off in pursuit of the Macdonnells. The marauders who had chosen the Inverness escape route were first to be trapped. They were caught three miles west of the town in a tavern. Barring all exits, the Mackenzies set fire to the inn and put to death 37 of those who had burned down the chapel. Poetic justice, indeed.

The other party soon faced retribution too. By the evening several had fallen to the swords of the Mackenzies. Next morning the captain and the remnants of his party were sighted climbing the southern ridge of Glen Urquhart. They dispersed on the order "Every man for himself." The captain doubled and redoubled on his tracks to shake off his pursuers, but it was not to be. They were still hot on his trail as he neared the ravine at Aultsigh. Throwing off his plaid and buckler and defying the leader of the Mackenzies to follow him, to took a run and made a desperate attempt to leap the chasm. Amazingly he cleared the gap.

The Mackenzie leader, not to be outdone, also leapt for the other side. Brave and determined, he was nevertheless not stimulated by the same feelings as his adversary and he could do no more than grasp a shoot of hazel as he reached the other side. There he hung helplessly until the captain, with a swift blow from his sword, severed the hazel and sent the helpless Mackenzie to his death far below. The captain had but a brief respite. More Mackenzies caught up with him, and one of them wounded him with a musket shot.

Losing blood and strength, the captain staggered on toward Loch Ness and plunged in to attempt an escape by swimming. Had it not been for the shouts and shots from his pursuers he might well have drowned. But the sounds reached Fraser of Foyers on the opposite bank. Seeing an armed band on the shore and a single swimmer struggling in the water, he sent out a boat to the rescue. To his amazement he discovered the man to be Allen Dubh, with whose family Fraser was on terms of friendship. Thus was the

Macdonnell's captain rescued from the point of death. He remained with Fraser until his wound healed and in due time returned to his clan.

This is but one of the stories of dark deeds of vengeance that are in Highland memory. If we think they were terrible and ferocious days, we are surely right.

But has not this horrifying episode at Cilliechriost a latter-day parallel in the records of Nazi atrocities during the Second World War?

Times change?

❖❖❖

The Longman trading estate, Inverness, a thriving and busy industrial complex, once contained three farms: the Citadel, the Seafield and the Millburn. On the west side of the town there was a big farm at Dalneigh — where they also made fishing rods. Other extensive farms in Inverness were at Kessock; at Carse, near the canal; and at Hilton.

Potatoes grew where Thistle now play

WHEN I was a child there were fields of potatoes and turnips near the Thistle football ground in Inverness. Our parents would buy a drill of potatoes and turnips during autumn for winter use. The price was quite reasonable, about 3d a yard for potatoes. Families would book a "hurlie" and on October holiday or preceding days we would all set to work to gather the crop. On an average, each family would gather five bags of potatoes during a forenoon. We would take them home and pass on the "hurlie" to the next family.

I clearly recall that when all our bags were placed on the "hurlie" I as the youngest, would be lifted to the top of the pile by my father. I was simply delighted to be sitting up there as we were homeward bound, my father and brothers singing "Cockles and mussels alive 'o!" My mother always had a grand special meal when we arrived home at night. One I liked very much was sliced sausage, onions and slabs of fried potatoes. We were tired but we certainly earned and enjoyed such wholesome rewards.

As a child I liked learning from my mother how to make girdle scones, pancakes, pastry and watching to see how she made potted meat with a large ham bone. Very tasty during summer, cold and jellied, with potatoes and veg.

Our summer holidays were usually special outings such as spending a day on the Black Isle. We would settle on a suitable place past the lighthouse where we could paddle, or collect whelks and little crabs, while our parents made a fire and filled a kettle with spring water. That tea tasted good to us all, with sandwiches and home-baked scones and biscuits.

On other days we would walk to Culloden to the "Clootie well." There we would tie a cloot to a nearby tree and make a secret wish.

On Sundays we all went to church, had a good dinner and then washed up the dishes while mother had a rest. Then we left to visit

116

our grandparents who lived in Kingsmills Road. We often found Grannie reading her Bible and had to remain quiet until she had finished. To pass the time we kept making faces at each other and kicking each other's legs under the table.

As a family we all had our house duties. The boys had to cut sticks; clean out the chickens' nests and change the water; and weed the garden. The girls had to scrub the doorsteps; clean the windows and brasses; polish the fireside; and clean out drawers and shelves. On Saturdays I also polished my parents' and brothers' shoes in readiness for Sunday. They were all lasting and satisfying duties that taught us to help each other in our home.

As old people who have experienced the horrors of two terrible wars, we always recall the years of our youth and home life and are grateful. We lived such happy lives in mutual service to our parents. The strong and lasting principles and loyal love helped us to adjust to and accept a changed form of living — but the memories of our youth we shall cherish for ever!

Soldiers were heard but not seen

A REGULAR annual visitor to John O'Groats, Mrs Helen Dove, of Morecambe, has vivid memories of Caithness going back over 80 years.   Early in 1975 she gave this interview to the 'John O'Groat Journal':

Many are the holidays that I have spent in Caithness.   The first one I remember was in the late 1890's when I was about six years old.   I came with my father and mother from Bingley, Yorkshire, to visit my grandmother, the widow of Rev. Roderick MacGregor, late of Canisbay Free Church.

My grandmother and her youngest son, David, lived in Argyll Square, and I think Dr. Banks lived next door.   While staying there I was taken ill and while recovering I remember music being played outside.   Maggie Fraser, who had been with my grandmother for some years, told me it was the Soldiers' Volunteer Band and that they wore red coats.   She said that when I was well she would take me to see them drill.

A few days later we heard the music again; Maggie hurried to help me with my coat but by the time we got outside, the soldiers had gone.   I never did get to see them in their red coats.

Another holiday in 1902, a few months after my father died in Bingley, my mother, my two older sisters and myself arrived in Wick after a train journey of over 20 hours.   The Barrogill Mail Coach was at the station with Archie McCleod — the driver for so many years.   He would take the mail to the post office for sorting.   When that was done and the mail bags for village post offices were on top of the coach, we embarked and set off on the 18-mile drive to John O'Groats.

On approaching Keiss an extra horse was attached to help up the hill.   Auckengill was the next village — here were the roadside stables where the two weary horses were changed.   After passing

118

through the village of Freswick, the road forks to the left, the direct road to John O'Groats was not completed. At this time it was known as the Red Road, I suppose because of the red sandstone surface.

On to what is known as "Maggie's Corner." Many years ago there was a public house kept here by the Cruickshanks. A daughter, Camilla, married Walter Ross who farmed the Glebe for the Free Church minister and drove the conveyance for him. (Mrs Walter Ross lived to a great age and has many descendants in the district.)

At "Maggie's Corner" there is a bridle or cart track which was known as the "Captain's Road." It was said to be made by my great-grandfather, Captain S. Sutherland of Brabster House and later of West Canisbay. It was made of imported stone so that a wheeled vehicle could go for peats instead of them being carried on the people's backs.

At this corner, the road straight on goes to Thurso but the coach turns left down the hill for Canisbay, Huna and John O'Groats. Here we alight for Pentland View to spend our holiday with our uncle and aunt, Dr and Mrs MacGregor. Two other visitors were there for a short time, they were musicians from London.

A concert was hurriedly arranged to take place in Canisbay School. Mr Wilfred James of Trinity College, London, and a member of the King's Private Bands, gave violin and bassoon solos accompanied by Mrs James, who also gave vocal solos. Dr MacGregor sang "The Boys of the Old Brigade." A duet was sung by the Misses McKenzie of the John O'Groats Schoolhouse. Rev. J. R. Forbes took the chair. The entrance fee was 6d and the school was packed to its full capacity. When the boys at the back applauded and stamped their feet too loudly, Mr Munro, the schoolmaster, stood up and shouted to them, "Will ye no' stop your capers?"

The proceeds were given to the fund for building the Gills Bay Pier.

This year, 1902, being the coronation of King Edward VII, a celebration for school children was held; sports were arranged and tea and buns were given. As everyone knows, owing to the King's illness, there was some doubt — however, all went on as arranged.

My two sisters and our two young Sutherland cousins on holiday from Edinburgh gathered large bundles of poppies, vetch and marguerites — red, white and blue — and decorated the gate of Pentland View (now a youth hostel).

119

We five young girls used to play on the beach at Huna. I could not walk, having had polio, but a wheel-chair was borrowed so I did not miss the fun. One day there was a lifeboat practice, the sirens sounded and the men were soon on the scene. I think Mr John Dunnett of Seater was coxswain, Willie Dunnett, known as "Postie," and probably Sandy Gunn of John O'Groats were members of the crew. It was a great thrill as the lifeboat went down the slipway, making a huge spash as it entered the sea.

Three Misses Davidson lived in a cottage still standing near the boathouse. They sold sweets and chocolate. We often went to speak to Kitty, the one who was an invalid, always in bed, and who did such beautiful embroidery.

The mail boat crossed from Huna to Stroma twice a week, taking goods of every description. Miss Ina Sutherland was the Huna postmistress for over 50 years. Her brothers and their sons worked at the blacksmith's nearby.

On our way from Canisbay to Huna I remember seeing Mr William Kennedy in his garden with a net over his straw hat as he attended to his bees. We did enjoy the honey in the comb that he gave us.

Many are the dear friends now gone, whose descendants I like to think of as my friends.

As a very small girl, I remember visiting old Mrs Kennedy in her cottage near the sea at Newton — her four dear daughters were close friends of all my people and myself.

For many years I have enjoyed the warm hospitality of my kind friend Mrs McKenzie at John O'Groats Hotel and later of her daughter at Seaview. In 1974 my grand-daughter and great-grand-daughter went with me and this year I hope to bring two other grandchildren with me.

Christmas was for the gentry

IN MY youth only the "big hoose" gentry celebrated Christmas. Celebrations for us farm folk were at New Year. Well I remember the sense of excitement and expectancy that hung in the air.

There was a general bustle of cleaning. First chimneys were swept in preparation for Santa. Curtains and screens were washed, starched and ironed. Grates were black leaded and the steel polished till it shone like silver. Knives had to be cleaned on a board with bath brick. This chore needed plenty of elbow grease. On Hogmanay a tray was set with whisky poured into a decanter; beside it a pretty plate with "sweetie" biscuits. On another, shortbread and black bun. Yet another held small portions of cheese.

We bairns were allowed to stay up till 12 o'clock to take in the New Year. Oft I'd wondered what it would look like. Suddenly we would hear voices and a tramping of feet and someone playing a melodeon. The door would burst open and everyone was shaking hands and wishing each other a happy New Year. Drams were passed round; toasts were given; songs sung; stories told. To the strains of the melodeon an eightsome reel would start up; followed by strip-the-willow, quadrilles and a highland schottische. After tea it was off to bed for everyone as we had to be early astir on the first day of the year. Mother was happy if we had been first-footed by a tall, dark man. He brought in a piece of coal and a bottle of whisky. Sometimes both. Finding an apple, an orange and some new pennies in our hung-up stockings made our New Year!

Fascination
of Cawdor

CAWDOR village has been described by some writers as the prettiest village in Scotland. It certainly has an old-fashioned glamour of its own. It's a homely community, indeed, but perhaps we can expect little else. because it's a place with a common interest — the Cawdor estate.

Until the 14th century the Thanes of Cawdor lived in the Castle of Nairn, with a small country seat at Old Calder, about half a mile north of the present Cawdor Castle. Early in the next century, William Thane of Cawdor was page to James II, and later became a king's favourite, rising to the position of Chamberlain for the King north of the Spey besides other honours. His carefully kept books are still preserved in the castle, it is said.

According to an old document dated 1454, we learn that Thane William was granted a licence to build a castle at Cawdor with walls, moats and iron portcullis, and to fortify it with turrets and other defensive ornaments and apparatus. The licence granted, where would he build? His answer was not only original but unique.

Placing a gold chest, containing the workmen's wages, on the back of a donkey, he set off the little grey animal to choose its own site, and according to tradition he decided to build the castle where the donkey rested. Under its heavy weight the donkey did not travel very far, and when it came to three thorn trees, it selected the middle one and lay down beside it; and there; around the thorn tree, Thane William built his castle.

Down in the basement or dungeon the little thorn tree is protected by an iron railing and the gold chest beside it! Ten years after building the castle Thane William died.

By the end of the 15th century the Thanes of Cawdor had become the most influential and richest family in Scotland, but constantly at feud with their neighbours, particularly the Roses of

Kilravock. In 1492 a grandson of Thane William (who built the Castle) married Isabel, daughter of Kilravock, but their first child died in infancy. The father died before the birth of the second daughter Muriel, and this young lady appears to have been the cause of a great upheaval in the family through no fault of her own.

At this stage Campbell of Argyll got himself appointed co-guardian of Muriel (then in infancy and heiress to the Cawdor estate) with Lady Kilravock. In 1499 he sent Campbell of Inverliver, with sixty men, to carry off the child. The grandmother, realising the motive of the abduction, and fearing trickery on the part of the Campbells, thrust the key of her coffer into the fire and branded the child on her thigh for future identification of the proper heiress. An alternative tradition states that the child's nurse bit the tip off a finger.

The baby was seized and despatched, in the care of six men, ahead of the main body of invaders, while the others dawdled in the rear with a dummy — a sheaf of corn disguised as the child. Soon Alexander and Hugh Calder, uncles of the babe, with a strong force caught up with the Campbells and a fierce battle ensued in the neighbourhood of Daltullich; but the child escaped unharmed with her abductors. In 1510, Muriel Calder married Sir John Campbell at the tender age of thirteen, and lived happily ever after. So the Campbells came to Cawdor.

The first Baron Cawdor rose to that honour in 1796.

To most local people, the strangest fact about Cawdor is that most visitors are astonished to find that it is all real . . . and not a fiction created by William Shakespeare!

123

Routes linked
with history

THOUGH with the building of the Cathedral at Fortrose, Rosemarkie's importance as an ecclesiastical centre waned, it must have remained a place well known to travellers from the south who had to cross by ferry to Chanonry Point and pass through Rosemarkie before moving on northwards.

From the ferry the traveller would come along the east side of the Ness, past a stretch of common called the Links which until recently extended to the bottom of the bank on which modern bungalows now stand, and behind which the land spread out in an amazing pattern of long narrow roods. Once in Rosemarkie he would no doubt seek refreshment in one of the many alehouses which were reported to exist there, or even, in more recent times, have put up at Miller's Hotel — which stood on the spot where an old coaching inn with ample stable yards must have been.

From the village the main route to the north crossed the ford at the Markie Burn, wound up past Kincurdy where Curitan's chapel may have been, followed a line parallel to the present road above the Fairy Glen before going over the hill in an almost straight line and down to Balblair ferry. From there, long ago, a pilgrim would have crossed on the next stage of his pilgrimage, perhaps westwards, as far as the shrine of St. Monan at Applecross, or, if the traveller were a chapman or trader, to the hamlets dotted along the sheltered northern shore of the Cromarty Firth. Another road led off this main route and crossed the old Eathie ford to Cromarty from where ferries crossed to Nigg and Tain.

In more recent times, the older inhabitants will tell you, London steamers bound to and from Inverness, called at the ferry pier to pick up or drop passengers and goods and certainly, before the days of the Black Isle Railway (whose terminus was Fortrose and which is now permanently closed) passengers for the south and east from the Black Isle and points north which were served by other convenient ferries, used the Chanonry ferry route to Gollanfield Station on the Inverness side of the Firth where they joined their respective trains.

It is interesting to speculate on the important part played by the Chanonry ferry in the economic life of Rosemarkie. Though there is no longer a ferry boat, it is not so many years since the pier at the Point was still a busy spot and the centre of the salmon fishing industry on which so many of the inhabitants depended for a livelihood. The following description passed on by word of mouth best illustrates the sort of activity there was at the Point right up to the last century —

"When I took my first trip south as a boy with my father who was coachman to the late Mr Fletcher of Rosehaugh's father, we embarked at Chanonry Point, machines, grooms, etc. At the same time all the salmon netted in the district were being sent south to Billingsgate and empty fish boxes and stores were being disembarked". At this time there were at the Point two ferrymen's houses, smoking or kippering sheds and an ice house for storing the fish.

Curious to think that at one time and that not so very long ago — when a farmer feed a salmon fisher to work for him during the closed season he had to undertake "to feed him on salmon on *only* one day a week and that day to be the Sabbath". There were indeed more salmon netted than could be eaten locally and icehouses had to be built for storing the fish which in those days sold at 3d per lb! But the upper proprietors of fishing rights on the Beauly Firth became worried about the effects on their own fishings of so much netting round Chanonry and, so the story is told, they managed to have the netting stopped with the help of river pilots from Kessock who swore on their oath that they had made tea from fresh water from a channel off the Three Burns near Cromarty, thereby proving that the rivers of the upper Firth still flowed freely as far out as that! The proprietors having thus successfully extended their riparian rights, declared that salmon had to be fished for only from cobbles and no longer netted — a method which threw quite a few fishermen out of work.

But salmon was even then so cheap — 1/- per lb. — that the proprietors of the rivers entering the Beauly Firth became worried because of the effects on their rod-letting of the sale of cheap salmon. They formed themselves into a company and bought out the lower proprietors thereby also terminating the leases of the salmon fishers of Rosemarkie and bringing the old industry to an end and the kippering sheds at the Point and the ice-house stood empty, and there were no longer any cobles drawn up near the salmon fishers' hut on Rosemarkie Beach and no more ice was made in the "Ponds" in the Fairy Glen for the ice-house near Kincurdy.

As an off-shoot perhaps of the salmon fishing industry, boat building was carried on in Rosemarkie last century. Naturally the cobles were made locally but boats, even of the schooner class, were built in a yard on or about the site of Tigh-na-mara. The most famous of these was the Louisa, built of larch from local woods and launched at Rosemarkie in 1852. Adjacent to the boat building yard there was a "Ropery" and yet another ice-house.

Many elderly local inhabitants remember much of the story of the ending of the salmon fishing and the gradual decline in the use of Chanonry Point, caused partly by extensive road-building, partly because of the development of the railways, partly by the silting up of Fortrose Harbour and the area of the pier at Chanonry Point, and finally by the death, by drowning, of the ferryman in 1938.

Now they look out to sea at ships which pass by Chanonry Point: cargo ships and tankers which ply to and from Inverness; small fishing boats out from Avoch whose dancing lights twinkle like hob-goblins in the darkness when they are fishing at night for the sprats and small Kessock herring for which the Firth is noted and which are pounced on by gulls, cormorants, porpoises and even the occasional seal. They have seen fishery cruisers and N.A.T.O. corvettes sail up the Firth and have watched warships of all kinds steam round the Sutor into the safe anchorage beyond Cromarty. But there is one ship they remember especially well — the Queen's yacht Britannia — which sailed past the Chanonry Lighthouse on the Point to pick up the Queen off Inverness after her visit to Ross-shire and the other northern counties — and then in the hours of early light sailed back again and out to sea — a graceful ship for a graceful lady.

Great days at Strathpeffer

"THE SEASON" in Strathpeffer at the beginning of the 20th century lasted from May to October and everyone living in the spa village worked terribly hard all through those months.

Ladies and gentlemen of quality arrived once a week on the L.M.S. train, 'The Strathy' direct from Euston to Strathpeffer. Trains from various places arrived at Strathpeffer almost every hour. A charabanc driven by a man in livery went to collect the clientele from the train.

Two doctors, brothers named Fox, brought patients to Strathpeffer through the summer and themselves spent the winter in Milan. The "cure" was never less than three weeks, more usually six weeks of baths and massage.

In the First Class and Second Class Pump Rooms there were sulphur baths and peat baths. Crofters came down from the hills above the Spa with peat for the peat baths. It was a very modern bath which was installed in the early 1900s.

Apart from "the quality" many people came for the cure. They stayed in hotels and boarding houses throughout Strathpeffer.

In the Square, people who owned garages all had a stance with a board in front proclaiming the pleasure runs for the day. Before the motor charabancs there were Victorias (one-horse carriages) and 4-in-hands. A favourite trip for the afternoon was to the Black Rock, Strathconon up by Achilty, over the black bridge and tea in the Strathconon Inn.

The chalet at the top of Knockfarrel was an octagonal timber tea-room with a table in each of the eight sides looking out of the window.

In Strathpeffer, every day, a band played on the bandstand from 11 a.m. to 1 p.m. and again from 3 p.m. to 6 p.m. The BeKay band from London came to Strathpeffer in 1908 and played in one hotel or another every evening — they were a five-piece band.

Year after year the same ladies and gentlemen would "send word" that they were coming for the cure and would stay at the address they always used. It is said that one couple came for 44 years without a break.

"The quality" had all their own cars and chaffeurs and between taking the waters and listening to the band they drove all over the west coast.

Each morning at 7 a.m. the piper would march all round the houses to waken everyone with stirring Scottish tunes.

The Highland Hotel was the first to be built followed by the Ben Wyvis and the Spa Hotel which was very grand. One year Queen Mary's mother, the Duchess of Teck, planted a tree at Strathpeffer. (Queen Mary was the wife of King George V).

One person who had to meet the morning train was the newspaper girl. They were a heavy parcel and Strathpeffer so hilly that she used to hide the bundle of papers under the mailbags, which were going to the post-office, to save carrying them.

Strathpeffer was very prosperous up to the First World War. In the "quiet months" the women mended the linen and carpenters, plumbers and painters did all the work for which there was no time between May and October.

Apart from the compact town of Strathpeffer there were only a few crofts — where the golf course is now. Old residents feel that housing estates have spoilt the character of the Spa town.

It is so sad that the once vital railway is now non-existent, its track a wilderness and that there is no longer the heavenly fragrance of baking bread when a quartern loaf was 9d and the buns melted in the mouth. The man who played his accordion sitting on a three-legged stool in the Square is only a memory, too.

Memories of the old "smiddies"

THERE WERE no chestnut trees, but there were a few "smiddys" (blacksmith shops) around Thurso in my young days. I particularly remember one which was on the site which is now Robert Dick Place as I lived in that area during the early part of my life.

This "smiddy" was occupied by the late John Waters and he didn't seem to mind the wee laddies hanging around watching him at work from a safe distance. We would marvel at this strong-armed moustached figure in shirt sleeves with perspiration running down his face as he hammered a strip of metal on the anvil, quickly shaping it into a horse-shoe. Sometimes we would become bolder and he would invite us to pump the bellows, which made his forge roar sending sparks up the chimney. As the metal cooled the blacksmith would return it to the forge then withdraw it white-hot, then more hammering on the anvil, sparks cascading around him.

The horse to be "shoed" is brought into the smiddy. We back to the furthest corner in apprehension at the sight of this massive Clydesdale. We now watch fascinated as the blacksmith turns his back and lifts the horse's leg placing it between his knees and proceeds to remove the old shoe. We see him trimming the hoof and wonder why there is no blood! The new shoe is placed on the hoof, the blacksmith finds he will have to make a slight alteration so he returns the shoe to the forge. A little more hammering then he places the shoe on the hoof. There is a sizzling, a white smoke engulfs the "mannie" and a stench of burning hoof permeates the smiddy. The horse doesn't seem to mind and we wonder why he hasn't reared and kicked.

Next to the smiddy was Jock Mackay's yard. On market days farmers would leave their horses and carts there. The horses would be unyoked and left in a field nearby. One particular incident which

129

my parents have related to me a few times happened when I was only four and a half and my "accomplice" James Banks was four. There are short chains which attach the horse collar to each shaft of a cart. They are called "pullers". My pal and I unhitched the "pullers" from the carts and hid them in all types of receptacles — in a barrel of tar, in drains behind sheds — devilment at that age! You can imagine the pandemonium of the owners of these carts when they arrived from the market!

A few were found but some farmers had to make do with bits of rope. Where were the culprits? I was told that old Jock Mackay — the owner of the yard — came charging into our house shouting: "Where is that little so-and-so?" Me? I was under the bed and when discovered, was sound asleep oblivious of the chaos we had created. They kept a strict watch on us after that! However, some time later. I appropriated Edward Mackay's hammer and was busy breaking stones, when I got a "dunder on 'e loog" and the hammer was snatched from my hand. One lesson I never forgot!

My father brought us a billy-goat as a pet, which we kept in the back yard. The children in the area would come around to feed it and of course to have the thrill of being chased by "Billy". He seemed to eat anything including a liberal amount of newspapers. When my parents discovered me satisfying his appetite with newspapers they realised that it was time he had a change of environment! Some readers will remember that white billy-goat proudly leading the Templars and Lifeboat fancy dress processions about 1923-24. I shouldn't have missed him so much as his main target seemed to be my bottom.

School was a smell of varnish

MY FIRST day at school remains a clear memory. It was a combination of claustrophobia; silence broken only by the teacher's voice; and the smell of varnish.

Early lessons were to repeat the alphabet and then to draw lines and loops on a slate. A spit and a wipe of the sleeve obliterated the wobbly creations, and the slate was ready for use again. How economical that was! Will the cost of paper and materials bring back the slate and the squeak of the slate pencil to the schoolrooms again?

The infants' lady teacher was a patient and forbearing lass. How different from the tyrant we encountered when we eventually qualified for the "Big Room." He was severe on the boys who forgot and had to be told again, and used the strap without mercy. Ten strokes was the common punishment for the least mistake. When he left the room he would select a boy to note down the "talkers."

This was a miserable dilemma for the unfortunate lad. If he did note down the talkers he was "in for it" at playtime. If he showed the master a blank slate he would get a walloping for not doing as he was told. Then, to our delight, this detested man was transferred to another school. He was replaced by a master who, although firm, was gifted with a sense of humour. "Oh that an angel would come down and throw some *light* on your benighted intelligence!" was his favourite exhortation. "Jerusalem artichokes!" and "Blue butterflies!" expressed his astonishment at "crass ignorance." But he was a good teacher and he produced good writers and scholars.

The playground was a stony brae flanked by a burn. The burn was the "loo" for the boys. Girls went to the wood or the hillside. Play not infrequently developed into clod-fights between the boys of

131

Corpach and the boys of Banavie.   Wet clods from the side of the burn was the ammunition . . . and NO STONES was the stern rule.

When summer holidays came we burst out of the schoolroom door, ran down the brae, threw pencils, rubbers, slates, etc., over the hedge into a field.   This was an unalterable rite and a joyful ceremony.

The day I was 14 I would not go back to school although urged to do so.   I wanted to work, as we were very poor, and within the week I got work with a nearby crofter.   After six months' toil I was rewarded with £4 and a new bonnet.

❖❖❖

If you think of an earwig as a ghooluchan, and are not sure how it is spelt, and think of other strange childhood names for ordinary things, it is possibly because only Gaelic was spoken in the house where you were brought up.   These childish names stem from the Gaelic.

People who went to school after the Great War were taught only in English.   Their parents and grandparents spoke the Gaelic but the native language was frowned upon by educationalists of the 1920s to the 1940s.   Now they are trying to undo what can now be seen as a bad mistake.

The Salvation Army picnic

HOT days bring my boyhood memories flooding back. This was the time when we took the opportunity of getting around in our bare feet. Oh, no! — times were hard in the late twenties and early thirties — but we weren't that hard up! It seemed to be the local custom that the boys went around in their bare feet or at least without stockings. At the beginning, we would be "hirplan" over the coarse ground (not many tarred roads in those days) but by the time the summer school break was over we could walk over anything without a wince!

One never sees the youth of today make use of our beach as then. Games such as "Quoits" using round flat stones, "Crobbie Fechts" and "Skintan Poolies" to mention only a few. Perhaps we went exploring the small caves, wandering over the rocks and perhaps gathering "wilks" and making a small fire and boiling them in a can of seawater. Do I perceive a cynical smile from our offspring? It may seem laughable and time-wasting to them but I assure you these were happy days and we were contented.

Delinquency? That word was never used. "Devilment," yes, but then we didn't think the occasional raid on the gardens, when the gooseberries were ripe, was anything but fun and when we were occasionally caught we took our medicine which was soon forgotten. Sergeant Watt and his stalwarts always seemed to find us (they didn't have radar but what a sixth sense!) We enjoyed a chase and the writer felt the weight of Constables Sinclair and Green's canes more than once.

There was an annual outing which stays fresh in my mind and it was looked forward to, by old and young. The Salvation Army picnic. Banniskirk — Westfield — Crosskirk — Dunnet Sands, a change of venue every year. Picnic morning. All concerned, up bright and early and "raring to go." Armed with the precious ticket and cup, parents and children make their way to the Army Hall. The contractors' horse-drawn lorries are already assembling (one never thought of the extra work put in such as fresh-painting of vehicles and polishing of harness). Long forms (seats) are roped on to the lorries. The officers, Miss Annie Sinclair, Peggy Mackay, John Sinclair, Walter Leed, to mention only a few, are already arranging the children on the lorries. How these people worked for the enjoyment of the children, down the years.

All aboard! Johnnie Sinclair in the lead with his white horse and "spring cartie" flying the Salvation Army Flag. Signal to start! Cheers! Handkerchiefs waving, an Army chorus begins on one of the lorries, rising to a crescendo as the occupants of the other lorries join in. Householders on the route, come out to wave and cheer us on our way. It is strange — open lorries — and I never remember a wet day at an Army picnic!

Arriving at our destination, we see smoke coming from an open fire in that field. The tall figure of "John" is seen among the people bustling around the fire (how did he get there before us?) preparing large urns of tea. Large boxes are stacked around containing those mysterious "baggies" which will eventually be distributed among us. Our eyes take in everything as we draw up around the field. "Take your time," "Watch 'at bairns," "Stay here," the orders are shouted thick and fast, as there is a rush of eager children dismounting from the lorries. Teachers and adults have made some semblance of a queue. "Line up now!" "Tea is ready," "Watch now 'ids hot," "Blow on 'id" as each "cuppie" is filled and the bags of cakes are handed out. Away we go in groups to consume our first meal. That long open air trip fairly gives us an appetite and the eatables soon disappear.

The programme of races is now being organised, heats have to be run; the competition is terrific, eventually the winners are announced and presented with their prizes. A few ball games now, several groups go on a short walk until the next round of tea and "bunnies." How time flies! Time now to tidy up, everybody joins in to pick up papers, etc., and leave the field in a clean condition. We may want to come back to this area again some time!

All aboard! There doesn't seem to be much enthusiasm now. An Army chorus starts up as the lorries begin their long haul to Thurso, "We're on the homeward trail." The journey seems longer, however, eventually we arrive at the hall. Parents are waiting, then home to bed, tired and happy, after one of the highlights of the year.

Village of many crafts

SALMON fishing was not the only industry in Rosemarkie. The first statistical account of 1794 showed a way of life which probably continued with little change for another fifty years until factory production drove the old shoemakers and weavers of Rosemarkie out of business. At that time, 1794, when the population was 296, there were merchants, shoemakers and their apprentices, linen weavers and apprentices, mill wrights, tailors, glovers (a really high-class occupation) and smiths, all plying their trades in the village, while those who were fishermen might also work on the land during the closed season.

The manufacture of linen began on a small scale about the middle of the 18th century and during the period from 1800 to 1830 there were about twenty weavers operating in their own homes. The flax was grown on the neighbouring farms and before being spun into thread, the lint was steeped in the man made ponds known to this day as "The Pows". They are situated in front of Fairy Glen House and the supply of water came from the Mill Lade above.

Perhaps the annual influx of cattle into Rosemarkie in early ages in payment of rents may have been the most important reason for the development of shoemaking, and as in Tain, the hides may have been required to be sent to local tanners. However, the trade developed and it was certainly an important one locally.

The shoemakers and the weavers sold most of their products at the various Fairs or Markets held yearly or half-yearly in every town or village in the Black Isle and some travelled as far as Dingwall and Inverness — walking all the way with their wares on their backs. Some of the linen was truly beautiful — one finely patterned example of a tablecloth is on display in the Highland Folklore Museum at Kingussie. The communion cloths still in use in Rosemarkie Church were woven from locally grown flax. The shoes were not of

135

such a high standard being rather disparagingly known at all the Markets as "Black Isle Boxies" because of their shapelessness. With the coming of the Industrial Revolution and the increased production of machine made goods both industries collapsed in time.

Nowadays there is no one particular trade in Rosemarkie although not so long ago there was still a shoemaker in the High Street who made his own shoes, and four tailors were fully employed in a shop in Bridge Street, the continuation of the High Street which leads to the Big Bridge over the Burn before the road climbs the hill to Cromarty and Balblair. There were also two mills functioning. Both are now private houses. But in the 1914 War blankets from Fort George were brought over to be washed in the mill stream, thus giving another instance of the to-ing and fro-ing that there was across the Chanonry Ferry. Many men once worked on the farms, since the greater part of the Burgh consists as it did in olden days, of agricultural land — but now, in this age of mechanised farming, only a handful of men are employed except at harvest and potato lifting time when extra "hands" are needed.

Many still remember the blacksmith who plied his trade near Courthill and who made horse shoes in the evening.

The witches of Forres

THE HIGHLANDS have had their fair share of witches throughout the ages and, in common with all mankind, the Highlanders have been known to deal with them summarily and hideously. Listen to this fearful tale of witchcraft near Forres . . .

There once lived in a castle just outside Forres a rich laird who had a young and beautiful daughter. As accomplished as she was attractive, this girl was understandably the darling of her father's eye. One spring morning as they were gazing contentedly on the scene which stretched before them from the castle, the girl drew her father's attention to the large number of ploughs which were at work on the estate.

"Indeed, there are many" he said, "and it is good to look upon them at work."

"Supposing if, by a single word, I should cause them all to become immovable," she said "What reward would you give me?"

Her father, astonished, laughingly replied: "If one word from you could cause all the ploughs to become still and the cattle to halt, I would give you the most costly and superb gown in all Forres."

"Very well," said the girl. She lifted her hand, uttered a low, unintelligible word and in an instant every plough but one stood stock still. Her father, understandably, was stupefied by astonishment. "That is incredible!" he exclaimed. "But there is one plough still working. Why should that be exempt?"

"I can easily guess," she said. "It will be because one of the oxen pulling that plough has a pin of the rowan tree. Such a branch defies all supernatural powers."

Her father was horrified. "Who taught you these things?" he demanded.

137

"My old nurse. Am I not deeply indebted to her for them?"

"Indeed you are, my child, and I shall soon see that she has her reward. Oh, my poor, dear daughter. Would that you had never been born."

Summoning a council of friends, the broken-hearted parent told them what had happened and sought their advice on what should be done. The council deliberated at length and finally decided that the girl was irrevocably lost to all good in this world. That being so, death was the only answer otherwise she would not only bring disgrace and infamy on her family and friends but would be doomed to eternal damnation.

The council therefore decreed that she must be put to death in private but that the nurse must be publicly burned under ignominious circumstance. This was a terrible decision for the father to accept, but he had no alternative. A doctor was called in from Forres to prescribe the easiest mode of death for the young girl. He advised bleeding as being certain, quick and painless. The girl was accordingly taken to an apartment in the castle. Seeing her father in an agony of tears, she ran to him in distress.

"Why are you crying?" she asked. "Have you had bad news? Tell me your sorrow that I may share it with you."

Before he could reply, the girl was torn from his arms, bound hand and foot and placed in a vat. The doctor plunged a knife in her veins.

"Do not kill me!" she screamed. "What have I done?"

But the agonised father had collapsed to the floor in his anguish. He did not hear his daughter's dying lament: "Do not kill me. What have I done? What have I done?"

The nurse, meanwhile, had been dragged from her cottage to the lawn in front of the castle. A huge fire of tar and other combustibles had been prepared and amid the curses and insults of the assembled throng she was thrown into it. As she burned, so the story goes, her body cracked like the sound of gunfire.

The story has several sequels. One which commends itself to many is the version which states that as the girl was bleeding to death it suddenly came to her that she had been guilty of witchcraft. Realising this, and remembering the men and cattle who were standing motionless in the fields because of her spell, she strove to utter the words which would release them. Unhappily she was able to release only some of them before life slipped away.

138

What happened to the rest? Well the story goes, they were turned into standing stones . . . which can still be seen not far from Forres.

It is not out of place to mention that not all witches were condemned to death in the Highlands. Some were saved by the process known as "Folorn Fire." This is what happened . . .

When witchcraft was diagnosed but the victim was not too far gone in evil to be beyond salvation. "Folorn Fire" was set up, Word was passed to all living within the two nearest running streams to extinguish all fires and lights on the appointed morning. Then the sufferer and his or her friends gathered around a spinning wheel, the intention being to work it so furiously that sufficient friction would be set up to ignite tow or some other readily combustible material. This was the "Folorn Fire".

Once the tow was alight, the flame would be passed to a candle. In turn the candle would ignite a fir-torch. The fir-torch would set fire to a cartload of peat which the master of ceremonies would distribute to messengers. They would run with it to different houses within the two streams to kindle the different fires.

By the influence of this operation, the power and spells of witchcraft were, to quote the legal phraseology of the day: "Rendered null and void; of no avail, force, strength or effect, with all that has followed or may follow thereupon."

There was yet another remedy for witchcraft known as the "Warlock's Stone." Legend has it that this stone was given by a mermaid to a Highlander to whom she had taken a fancy. A single immersion of it into a hogshead of water instantly gave the water such powers that one drop would cure the most desperate case of witchcraft in the Highlands.

Alas. There seems to have been such precipitate haste to apply tradition and well-tried exorcisms by fire when witchcraft reared its ugly head in a community that few had an opportunity to test the efficacy of the "Warlock's Stone."

Certainly not the laird's daughter at Forres. Nor her nurse.

The magic of Dunlichity

EVEN today the tiny village and district of Dunlichity, near Inverness, has a magical atmosphere of mystery, so it is small wonder that legends and stories abound.

In the year 1530, the barn of Tordarroch was the scene of rather a bloody massacre. It all started over a clan chiefship dispute between the Earl of Moray, acting on behalf of young MacKintosh, then not "of age," and Hector MacKintosh of MacKintosh. A meeting was called by the Earl of Moray to settle the dispute, and when his opponent's followers turned up for the gathering, eighteen of them were strung up from the rafters, giving rise to an old saying from the chance remark of one who was there:

"It's not everyday that MacKintosh holds a court"!

These are the facts contained in the History of the Clan Chattan, but local lore says that the actual number killed was fifty, and not eighteen. They were buried in Dunlichity Churchyard.

In the old days, a hand-bell was rung to summon folk to Dunlichity Church. It has an interesting story linked with it.

When plans were made to build the church the bell was taken there. It re-appeared, however, at Brinmore, some three miles away, now only the site of the former Church. Some folk thought that supernatural powers were at work, because every time it was taken to Dunlichity it re-appeared next day at Brinmore!

The Church built at Dunlichity in 1759 was the third to be placed on that site. A tradition says that a former building had a porch, where the men of the district left their bows and arrows during the services, and the marks of the sharpening of the arrows were seen on the porch door.

An interesting old stone tells rather a remarkable tale in itself—provided the facts carved on it are authentic.

It is to the memory of Alexander MacGillivray of Dalcrombie, who died on the 18th January, 1797, aged 38. Also his son, Donald MacGillivray, who died 18th September, 1797, aged 25.

That means the son was born when his father was only thirteen years old!

At the corner of the churchyard is the old watchtower, from where relatives of newly-interred corpses watched their graves against body snatchers.

Over a century ago an old meal mill stood in a field opposite Dunlichity Churchyard on the glebe ground. and in nearby Loch Chlachlain lies an ancient mill-stone, which never even reached its destination at the mill. It had been hewn out of rock on the hillside overlooking the loch, and rolled down some fifty yards, when it got out of control and finished its passage at the foot of the loch. I believe it can be seen lying at the bottom on a clear day, but nobody has managed yet to retrieve it!

On another rocky hillside, to the west of Loch Duntelchaig, one of the last wolves in Scotland was killed by a woman with a girdle in her hand. She had gone to Letterchullin from Dunchea, in Stratherrick, to borrow the girdle, met the wolf on her homeward journey, and consequently crowned it in self-defence!

Between Loch Ashie and Loch Duntelchaig is Fingal's Stone, where the famous Druid king is supposed to have watched the fray of one of his many murderous battles. Dotted about Ashie Moor are various tumuli, which obviously tell of bygone strife, and one particular heap of stones is supposed to represent the Castle of the King of the Sea — but little seems to be known of its significance.

It may have had something to do with the ghostly battle between ancient warriors, still reputed to be seen soon after dawn on a May morning. In 1870-1, the spectral fray was witnessed, and caused much excitement in the newspapers, as to whether it was a mirage of the fighting in France. The scenes have been very vivid — large bodies of men in close formation and smaller forces of cavalry facing an attacking army marching from the east; wounded men clapping spaghnum moss to their wounds and binding it on with strips torn from their shirts.

On one occasion a man cycling to Inverness saw three horsemen in front of him on the road. He followed for a distance, then, turning a corner, ran right into them, and to his amazement straight through them; falling off his bicycle in horror!

West from the cross roads, where the road verges into the Kindrummond road, you may be able to find an old well, called the Well of the Beard, so named because men drinking from it frequently dipped their beards into the water. One tale records that a bearded packman was murdered there, and that the spot is consequently haunted, giving rise to another possible name, the Well of the Spectre!

The doctor had been called to see Jenny who had a sore throat. Scarlet fever was diagnosed. Looking at Jenny's lovely golden hair spread over the pillow and two pairs of agonised eyes, doctor said to Mother — "Och! Soak a sheet in disinfectant and cover the doorway — you will be the only one to tend Jenny and wash all her cups, saucers, plates, etc. in disinfectant, also handkerchiefs and clothes, bedclothes and your own hands in disinfectant. It would be a shame to send her to the Fever Hospital where they would cut off all her hair."

There were many child deaths from scarlet fever 50 years ago.

Danger days
in Rosemarkie

BETWEEN the 9th and 12th centuries life on the Rosemarkie peninsula must have been hard and dangerous and Viking raids would have taken their toll. This was an age which gave birth to many sagas, a well-known one being the story of the battle which was fought between the Danes and the Scots near the grey cairn — Cairn Glas — at Blackstand on the ridge above Rosemarkie. When, early last century, one of the many cairns on the ridge was opened, human remains were found. There were stone coffins and weapons of copper and other metals and it was said that after a battle a huge Danish chief was buried there whose skull was said to be so gigantic as to contain "twa lippies of bear". After the Vikings the northern parts of the Highlands were involved in the long civil wars between the Gaelic descendants of Malcolm Canmore and his first wife and the family of his second marriage to the English princess, Margaret. It is believed that the rebellious people of the Moray Firth coast were transplanted and replaced by strangers from the south, Scots, English, Normans and a few Flemish. Whatever the truth of this may be, it is interesting to note that when written records became available for Ross-shire during the late 16th century, surnames and place names in the village and peninsula of Rosemarkie are found to be almost entirely non-Gaelic.

This disappearance of Gaelic speech would also have been brought about by the coming of English speaking priests from the south who, over the years, almost completely changed the character of the area. True, MacBeth, the first Bishop of Ross, created by David I had a Gaelic surname—but he seems to be the only one who had and it is likely that David at that time busily engaged in establishing the Catholic Church and the feudal system, as instruments of his policy for the pacification of the kingdom, may well have induced the abbots of what were then called Culdee Colleges to accept his

143

plan by installing them as the first Bishops of the Catholic Sees which appeared for the first time during his reign.

At this time Rosemarkie must have been dependent on the existence of the Cathedral there; the people probably worked to provide for the needs of the Clergy and for themselves, claiming even then on the Mulbuie — the wasteland behind the narrow fertile coastal strip of this part of the Black Isle, the right of "muir, moss and commonty" since to it the people, rich and poor alike, resorted for pasture for their cattle and fuel for their fires. Although there was virtually no trade with the outside world there would have been a lot of going and coming of kings and princes, pilgrims, churchmen, soldiers and pedlars, across the Chanonry Ferry which was the main route from the south — and possibly all would halt awhile in Rosemarkie for the latest gossip to be picked up about the church and fellow travellers before continuing their journey either north or west.

At one time the ferry which had linked the coasts of Inverness and Ross-shire at this Point for so many centuries, had carried men, sheep, cattle and later, horses and carriages and before that it must have carried pilgrims and all sorts of travellers, right up to recent years when the soldiers stationed at Fort George used to cross regularly to shop and to be entertained. But the ferry stopped running in 1938 and now all traffic goes the long way round by Inverness town and the Kessock Ferry. In the old days, before the road was built over the Grampians, the only route north from Edinburgh led, east of the mountains and over lower ground to Ardersier before crossing by the Chanonry Ferry. How busy it must have been long, long ago; how sad that, since the last ferryman was drowned, there should no longer be a ferry there.

The Danes had crossed the seas to come to this part of Ross and it was they who had given the Black Isle its name; the Black Isle, which is seldom black and is certainly not an island. It was said that when the Vikings conquered Ross-shire this part had been given by their chief to the black swarthy Danes and had become known as Tir'n Dubh Ghuile (pron. yuile—"the land of the Black Danes") —and through centuries of common speech, became simply Black Isle.

The march of time

LOOKING back to my boyhood over 70 years ago, what are the changes I see in my village of Corpach and the surrounding district?

Well, the solidly-built old school has gone, and in its place is a square glass and concrete structure with a fenced-in tarmac playground. How different from the green hillside open spaces where we played at "Hunting the stag."

No longer does one see on the main road a shepherd or drover leisurely driving cattle; or the slow horse and cart jogging along. A large part of an ancient fir wood has been sacrificed to widen the road for the benefit of coal lorries, cattle floats and endless streams of cars.

The crofters' peat banks have been bulldozed out of existence to make room for rows of houses. The picturesque old mill-wheel has long since gone to rest and a pulp mill has been erected near the dusty miller's old home. Even the wee sweetie shop, where we long debated how to spend our half-pennies, has been replaced by a self-service store.

Gone, too, are the days when hardy lock-keepers strained at the capstan bars — with sight-seeing tourists lending a hand to operate the heavy lock gates. A press-button operator now does the work of many hands. Gaelic speaking people are fewer in number as are the hard-working crofters. The noisy tractor has replaced the gentle horse. No longer is heard the sound of the reaper as he sharpened his scythe . . . and nor is the harsh sound of the corncrake.

However, we still have with us our Big Ben; the loch; the river and the shore to keep us old ones in touch with the days of long ago.

145

Inverness had a racecourse

DID you know that in the Dunain district of Inverness there used to be a rather splendid racecourse? It was opened on the flat east of Dunaincroy in 1823 by members of the Northern Meeting, but the original racecourse was situated around Tomnahurich Hill. In the 17th century horse racing was even more encouraged than it is today and in those times peers and chiefs rode their own mounts. The races were discontinued during the Commonwealth period, but re-established after the Restoration.

At a meeting held at Tomnahurich on the 24th and 25th May, 1662, amid a large attendance of earls, chieftains and barons, the Provost and Magistrates of Inverness, with the citizens, marched in procession to the town boundary, and, with the usual ceremony, hung high the Silver Cup and blue ribbons to be won, along with a saddle and sword. On the first day, the saddle, valued at £7, was won by Lord Lovat, while on the second day, one of the magistrates of the Burgh, Bailie Fraser, won the sword and cup. According to custom, the Laird of Glenmoriston purchased the winning horse for £13, rather on the lines of our modern "Selling Plate" handicaps.

An annual meeting was held at Dunain on the Saturday of the Northern Meeting week, which nearly everybody attended. Some of the best English ponies, many of them owned by local lairds, competed under the Pony and Galloway Racing Rules with the usual weights; but these events came to an end in 1914, and were never resuscitated.

The derivation of Tomnahurich is controversial. It may mean the hill of the boat, or the boat-shaped hill (as indeed it is), though another explanation is the Fairy Hill.

"Strange as it may seem to you this day," prophesied the renowned Brahan Seer, "the time will come — it is not far off —

when full-rigged ships will be seen sailing eastward and westward by Muirtown and Tomnahurich, near Inverness."

He was right again! The Caledonian Canal is the obvious answer.

The prophet then added, "that the day would come when Tomnahurich; or, as he called it *Tom nan Sithichean*, or "Fairy Hill," would be under lock and key, and the fairies secured within. As Tomnahurich is now a beautiful cemetery, it may be possible that the seer was referring to the dead bodies entombed therein.

Not far away, Dochgarroch House was the family seat of a branch of the Clan MacLean; and a member of this family, John MacLean, seems to have spent most of his life as an outlaw. His troubles started when he returned home from Killiecrankie. For his part in the fray he was outlawed and took refuge in Strathglass until the amnesty of 1693, when all who showed title deeds and took oath of allegiance to King William were pardoned.

However, John MacLean went out again in the 1715 Rebellion, and consequently was outlawed again, and his mother and brother installed in his place. Again, he was pardoned, and at this time he built the House of Dochnalairg, where he lived undisturbed and surrounded by his followers.

Unfortunately, a number of Hessian soldiers came into the neighbourhood for a foraging party, and began to help themselves. Whereupon, MacLean, with a handful of men, challenged them with sticks, actually killing one of the soldiers. For a third time the luckless laird sought refuge in the hills!

In 1740 he was persuaded to give himself up, but as no one would bear witness that he was responsible for the killing of the soldier, he was liberated and lived in peace for a few years.

Informality of
a dander

"WUR goan' a dander 'e day." Now-a-days it is called a ramble and is probably organised by a youth club. The aim was the same, except that we did not plan direction or distance, and only "hownger" gave us the knowledge that it was time we were "makan' for hom'."

Let us begin our route from Thurso Post Office and go by the "Royal." We see that one of 'e toffs has thrown away a cigar "stumpie," One of the party pounces on it — that will be handy for a sly puff later on. Further down Traill Street we pass the Meadow Well and see the "weel-kent" faces of Keena, Katie and the two Bellas, the group of fish-wives who display and sell their fish from the unique fish-baskets which they carry on their arms. I believe these baskets were unique, being used only in Thurso. A basket somewhat similar was used by Newhaven fish-wives, perhaps slightly deeper. Alas, time and woodworm have taken toll of these baskets and I am afraid they have all disappeared.

Continuing along Traill Street on to Rotterdam Street, probably named in recognition of many foreign sailors who frequented Thurso during the days of sailing ships and schooners when there were large exports of Caithness flagstone to all parts of the world.

Somebody has found an old tin can and, kicking the can around, we carry on to High Street to Willie Horne's shop to bargain for "chipped aipples" or broken chocolate. It was amazing the bargains we would get for a few coppers.

Around the corner to Swanson Street where we "splice" to buy a rubber ball from Finlay's wee shop. It only cost two or three pence and was probably a reject since it would stot in every way but the way it was supposed to!

On to the Esplanade "greenie" for a kick around with our new ball. A warning cry. "Here comes Skinner!" Mr Skinner was the Burgh Chamberlain and he took the task of keeping this green patch free of budding Jimmy McGrorys and Alan Mortons!

Let's get on our way — "Doon till 'e sand" — and have a game of "skintan poolies" using small, thin stones, we would throw them so as to skiff the top of the water, and the person who made the most "loups" over the water with his stones was the winner.

Along now to the "Clio", that is the triangular rock at the west end of the beach where the youngsters learned to dive and swim. When one was proficient, one advanced to the Rock-Well about a hundred yards further on.

Between the "Clio" and the "Rock-Well" there is a small cave called "Name-e-goe" — where there was a well-carved Salvation Army crest on the walls. Alas, time and water have done damage to the skilled work and patience of those Thurso youths who must have spent hours chipping the hard rock. Incidentally, during the early 30s there was a hardy bunch of gentlemen—average age 70 years — who had a daily dip, summer and winter.

We are now past the "Rock-Well" and search for some curious shaped rocks — the devil's kitchen — including the "Devil's spoon," the "Devil's bowl," etc. We are getting hungry and search around for "dilks" an edible sea-weed and "rake" for "wilks." We arrive at "Burnside" and collect some driftwood, get a fire going and proceed to boil our "wilks" in a tin can. "Clean meit never fattened 'e peeg" and it did us no harm! After our "meal" we light up the cigar "stumpie". The aroma! We pass it around, a puff each — everything shared equally. After our rest, we proceed along "Burnside" and pass "Bishop's Castle" ruins: only a mound remains now. On to Scrabster road where we turn left and along "Howe-burn" enroute to the golf course, chasing a "sheepie" or two on the way.

On arrival at the golf course we begin a search for golf balls. Should any be found we would take them home and "twite" the hard composition covering and reel out the yards of thin elastic which go to make up a golf ball, to find a small ball of white messy substance in the centre.

We are hungry again and find a field of "neeps" where we help ourselves to one each. The neep is bashed on the edge of a flagstone "dick." How we used to enjoy those neeps, our faces tingling with the acid juices. Our "bowgs" satisfied again, we wend our way to the "swinging breeg" and spend a "whilie" testing the strength of that bridge. No "bobbies" here to bother us.

Continuing along the riverside towards the "Mall" we perhaps attempt to climb some trees. Arriving in town, we find the shops are closed (we must be late). We now begin to hurry to our homes being met with the inevitable question, "Where hav' ye been? Yur denner has been ready ages ago." Our usual reply, "Oot playan," seemed to answer the question and perhaps it would be ages after when we might let slip about our "dander."

◆◆◆

When Willie or Margaret was told that their tonsils must come out, in the early 1920s Mother was ordered to scrub the kitchen table spotlessly clean (it was of wood) and have plenty of boiling water on the hob on the day when the doctor called at their home to take out the tonsils.

Bottle and rag took care of anaesthesia as the child lay unconscious on the scrubbed table top and the G.P.-surgeon proceeded to remove the tonsils in full view, and with the assistance, of the Mother.

Brief encounter

THE Drumochter pass on the A9 just south of Dalwhinnie is an area of wild splendour in the summer but it can be a white hell for drivers in the winter. For when all other roads in the Highlands may be clear, suddenly a blizzard can rage along the length of the Drumochter — and woe betide the road user then!

Should you happen to be driving along the Drumochter one evening when the weather is fine, and especially as dusk is closing in, pull into a layby, wind down your window and listen. Listen carefully . . . patiently . . .

During the rebellion of '45 in Prince Charles' retreat from Derby, the main body of his Highlanders were compelled, on their northward march through Badenoch, to make a short halt at Drumochter to enable stragglers to catch up. Being sorely harassed by a party of English cavalry, the Highlanders resented the Prince's stubbornness in not permitting them to tackle the horsemen forthwith. But the Prince had no relish for combat just then. His men were in a desperate condition because of the rigours of their journey and, he was sure, would be no match for fresh troops and horses. But his words were of no avail and his men determined to take matters into their own hands. They wanted to see the enemy dislodged from the hill and two clans, the Macdonald and the Macpherson, formed the assault party to move in on 600 English.

The battle commenced and was ferocious and bloody. The English in expectation of attack, had dug themselves in well. They defended resolutely but once the Highlanders, ignoring their many losses, had gained a foothold in the trenches it was all over. The English, acknowledging defeat, scattered and ran. They were pursued by the Highlanders who, in the fierce tradition of those terrible days, killed them all to a man. The last Englishman to die fell on the banks of what has been known ever since as the "Ault-na-Sassenach" or "Englishmen's burn." The spot where he fell is marked by an upright stone about 30 feet from the stream.

In all, the battle is said to have lasted less than an hour. It was not a historic victory. It neither changed the course of events nor constituted a landmark in the bitter struggles of those days. It was a brief encounter between men at the point of exhaustion and pursuers who must surely have felt that they had little to fear from an unkempt band of tired, hungry and thirsty stragglers. That was their mistake and it cost them their lives.

Now, nothing remains but a gaunt stone embedded in the moss a few feet from the stream. A few relics have been turned up from time to time — claymores, dirks, musket-barrels and so on. But nothing else is there to remind the modern traveller of a savage, sudden and merciless conflict between two brave and dedicated bodies of men when hatred and blind prejudice ruled all hearts.

Nothing?

As you sit in your car with your window wound down . . . listen. It is said, and has long been said, that at Drumochter at the hour of gloaming you might chance to hear the wailing of the pipes — but will find it impossible to tell where the melancholy strain is coming from. And as the piping fades, other sounds might come to your ears: the sounds of sword upon sword, the roll of muskets, the cries and groans of the dying.

More still . . .

Before the light finally goes it is said that those who have heard the sound of the pipes and the sounds of conflict will, if they strain their eyes, see the spectres of those who fell still engaged in ghostly combat; still fleeing from the vengeful Highlanders; still sinking to the blood-soaked ground of Drumochter.

Pull into that lay-by. You never know!

Wash day went with a bang!

WHEN one considers today's sophisticated laundering arrangements in the average home and then casts one's thoughts back to the wash-days of yesteryear, the miracle is that both the clothes **and** the laundress stood up to it! It was a hard experience for both of them.

In our household, wash day was always on a Monday and was usually heralded by a minor explosion as my mother got the fire going under the huge stone copper with the aid of a pint or so of paraffin. The copper had a large wooden lid with a wooden handle, and ready to hand was a big, wooden copper-stick . . . the use of which was not solely confined to wash day. I can still feel the weight of that copper-stick on my bottom!

When the water was nicely boiling, in would go the clothes: whites first, then coloureds. There was a formidable consignment of both, for there were no skimpy bras, wispy girdles and bare midriffs in those days! The average woman in late Edwardian times wore a vest, chemise, stays, camisole, drawers, petticoats (flannel and calico), woollen stockings, dress, and, indoors, apron or pinafore. Then, of course, there were the nightgown, night vest and, often, bedsocks.

The clothes weren't just boiled, either. They were scrubbed. This involved a wash-board (beloved of New Orleans jazz bands!) and, to start with, a bar of soap. The clothes were lifted from the copper on to the wash board and then scrubbed by hand with the bar of soap. Later the hand scrubbing brush came into use to make quite sure that everything was as clean as it should be. All this was performed in an atmosphere so steam-laden that it was hard to see across the kitchen.

The scrubbed clothes were then put through the mangle. This was a vast iron contraption with wooden rollers and a big handle

153

mounted on a wheel at the side. The rollers were compressed by screwing down a knob on the top of the frame. The tighter the rollers were compressed, the more water was squeezed out — but the more power was demanded on the handle. Frequently other members of the household were called in to do the mangling, either to save time, or more often, because my exhausted mother simply had not the strength left to do it.

After the soapy water had been mangled out, the clothes were dumped into a bath of rinsing water. This was cold water to which had been added the blue-bag — a little cube of blue substance tied up in a cotton cover. The miracle ingredient of the past! The blue-bag, incidentally, worked wonders with wasp stings . . or was it bee stings.

After rinsing, there was more mangling and then the clothes were hung on the line to dry. If it was raining, they were stood on a clothes-horse in front of the fire, to add their quota to the dripping humidity which now had spread throughout the house. Later, of course, came the ironing.

This was performed with a flat iron heated by standing it in front of the kitchen range. The correct temperature was indicated by the amount of sizzling when one spat on it. Absolutely everything was ironed: nothing was excluded. Some housewives used to mangle their sheets and towels flat to save ironing, but not my mother. Then, ironing completed, everything went back on the clothes-horse to be aired before the fire.

Sometimes there were wash day disasters. The worst — and it happened all too often — clothes pegs failed to keep items on the line and they would fall into the dirt. Sometimes there was real tragedy when the prop slipped or broke and **everything** went in the dirt. We children took good care to be on our best behaviour and to keep well clear on those explosive days!

154

It was "devilment", then

"DEVILMENT" covered quite a number of our escapades and the greatest fun was in being chased — and not being caught! The picture of innocence on our faces when we arrived home "saved our bacon" on my occasions. We would creep into our homes by the back door — to the sink in the kitchen — give our faces and hands a "dicht", then a voice from the living room "What are ye do-an?" "Notheen", was the usual answer. Then you made an appearance. "Where wis ye?" and the usual answers: "Oot playan", or "chist up 'e street". These replies seemed to satisfy, then supper and off to bed, perhaps to plan for the following night.

I remember on one occasion, along with two pals we went on a "gooseberry raid". Unknown to us, the owner was lying in wait to trap the unsuspecting. The first lad went through the opening in the hedge — called to us that the coast was clear, we made our way inside, and were grabbed by the owner, receiving a hefty "skelp" on the side of a head. The first lad was presented with a pocketful of gooseberries for his treachery! We had our share of the spoil before we "sent him to Coventry". On another occasion we had filled our pockets — except for one lad who had holes in his. However, "necessity is the mother of invention" so this lad rolled up the front of his "ganzie" (jersey) and used that for his berries. On returning from the raid we were passing the War Memorial — innocent as usual — when somebody remarked: "Herr's Watt, 'e bobby!" The lad who had stored the berries in his ganzie let the contents fall to the ground in his nervousness! I am sure the hundred yards' record was unofficially broken that night as we dashed down the street!

Before the era of electric lighting the streets of Thurso were dimly lit by gas lamps. These gas lamps were switched on or off by an employee of the Gas Company by means of a long pole moving a small lever. It was no bother to the "Thirsa boyagies" to shin up the lamp-post and switch off the light. No doubt many of our readers will remember this and, of course, the "coortin' couples" never complained. Although I took part in lots of the escapades I mention in my articles, I was innocent of many, so I hope the "powers that be" are not examining their old files!

Thurso Harbour was the port of call for small coasters delivering wood, coal, animal feeding-stuffs (yes, we'd have a taste of a "bittie" of oil-cake, also.) I remember, between the wars, the carriage of these commodities from the boat to their various destinations was by horse and cart. When the coal was being carted, one favourite trick was to place stones in the path of the wheels so that the inevitable bump would shake off a few lumps to the delight of the nearby housewives, the lads would snatch the fallen lumps and present them to the grateful "wifies". There was a man employed to deter this "racket". He was armed with a cane but was never quick enough to catch the culprits. Not delinquency — just devilment!

Many will remember the "Iron Hoosies" which were placed strategically around the town. These were made of cast iron plates, bolted together and were of elaborate Victorian designs perforated with small holes. The occupants of these "hoosies" were disturbed on many occasions by the "boyagies" squirting water through these small holes!

There was not much pocket money available for fireworks in those days but we used to give many people a "gluff" (fright) with our own home made "bangers". This was the days when carbide cycle lamps were in general use and we used to buy a few pieces of carbide for a penny. Our bangers were made from a syrup tin, a small quantity of water and a lump of carbide. The tin had a small hole punched in the bottom. A few drops of water were put in the tin, then the lid put on. A gas was formed by the water coming in contact with the carbide. A lighted match was then put to the hole and with the resulting explosion the lid blew off with a terrific bang. I notice that bird scarers are now made on the principle of our bangers!

Talking of fireworks, Guy Fawkes' night was not observed as it is today. We had more fun on "Hallowe'en Night". This consisted of dressing up with any old togs and soot on our faces. We then went from door to door asking "anything for Hallowe'en?" One received gifts of a few coppers, fruit, nuts or sweets. I note nowadays the children carry shopping bags with them. We were satisfied with the pockets of a "beeg owld jaicked" which was borrowed from an adult member of the family. There were some householders who did not welcome us and perhaps a pail of water was thrown on us from an upstairs window. That was asking for trouble! After we had finished our rounds we ganged together and got our own back in many ways which I shall leave to your imagination!

❖❖❖

She has lived many years in Inverness and is now grandmother to two lively schoolgirls but she has never forgotten the wonder and joy of a cycle ride along the track, it was no more, along Loch Ness side, through Dores, in April, when she was in her teens.

Primroses bloomed right across the track and at Inverfarigaig where the rock came right over to the edge of the loch there were icicles as thick and long as her fore-arm, sparkling like diamonds in the sunlight. It was fairy-land.

"Family" life in the croft

LOOKING at an old, deserted croft from the comfort of our car most of us wonder just what life was like in those tiny, remote and primitive dwellings. The answer is that it all depends.

Originally, it is likely that the most northerly crofts derived from the Viking longhouse and that people and cattle lived side by side, using the same door and separated inside the building only by a low stone wall. Poultry and pigs also shared the accommodation in what were frankly mean, dark and insanitary hovels.

Even at the end of the 18th century many crofts had no windows or, at best, a small hole in the roof. In the makeshift lamps, fish oil or mutton fat was used as fuel. Tallow candles did not come until much later.

In the mid-1800s chimneys and windows were in general use and the interiors were much more attractive and domesticated. Dirt floors had been replaced by flagstones — not infrequently cleaned with milk. There were wooden cupboards and furniture, and a spinning wheel was a "must."

For centuries oatmeal was the basic food, and this was supplemented by fish — in the coastal regions — and some green vegetables. Herrings became available to inland crofters early in the 19th century and were not infrequently dried for winter use. Potatoes appeared about 200 years ago; swedes came later.

Ordinary people customarily drank ale. Milk was certainly available but was generally made into cheese. Whisky was even more available! Distilleries abounded and parish records tell of excessive drinking all over the Highlands.

Most crofts had a few sheep which supplied the family with wool. It was one of the wife's many chores to weave the wool into cloth for clothes and blankets. These were generally of a dull, grey colour, but special clothes were dyed in various colours.

In the 18th century the customary footwear was "rillans" — light shoes made from untanned leather worn hairy-side out and held on by thongs. Not only were these shoes not waterproof, they often had holes punched in them to let the water drain out.

Crofters — like many of us! — were superstitious folk. Certain wells and lochs were held to have magical powers of healing, and curious rites and practices were invoked to lessen the risk of colds and rheumatism.

A receipted account from the Miller's Hotel on the Black Isle recently came to light. Among the items were the following: To one gill, 6d; one half-mutchkin, 10d; 3 gills, 1s 3d; 2 btls. whisky, 4s; 2 btls. ale, 1s.

ACKNOWLEDGEMENTS

How do you begin to thank an army? Collectively and anonymously? There would certainly be no objection to that from the army of people who, by their labours, their enthusiasm, their encouragement and their co-operation made this book possible. For the last thing they sought was acknowledgement. Indeed, most of them positively forbade it!

Help came in a hundred practical ways once I had declared in the Highland News Group of Newspapers my hope that readers would assist me to produce a book about memories and legends that should not be permitted to fade into oblivion. Articles, letters, phone calls and advice flooded in and I was soon submerged in an embarrassment of riches. What, then, to leave out?

That problem caused me more anguish than anything. My only comfort to those whose wonderful material had reluctantly to be placed on one side simply because one cannot squeeze a quart into a pint pot is that, who knows, I might have to produce a second volume before long.

Many people I cannot thank by name, for much material came in very anonymously indeed. Some I will name, — and I am mindful in advance of their inevitable disapproval! — are those listed herewith. My sincere appreciation to them all.

Mrs I. Baikie (Slough)
Mr Herbert Booth (Thurso)
Mrs M. Crawford (Rosemarkie)
Miss Jean Coutts (Caol)
Miss Helen Dove (Morcambe)
Mrs Ruth Gow (Inverness)
Mrs B. M. Jeffrey (Fort William)
Mrs Elizabeth MacGregor (Inverness)
Mr Darry Mackay (Inverness)
Mr William Mackenzie (Inverness)
Mrs S. Mackintosh (Inverness)
Miss Mary Macleod (Inverness)
Mrs D. Matheson (Dingwall)
Mrs Amelia McCorriston (Cannich)
Mrs Nola Miller (Gold River, British Columbia)
Mrs Marjorie Mitchell (Inverness)
Mrs Christina Morrison (Uig)
Mrs K. Palmer (Dagenham)
Mrs Ishbel Puliston (Inverness)
Mrs Mary Ralph (Inverness)
Mr W. S. Robertson (Inverness)
Miss M. A. Roloff (London SW18)
Mrs C. Wells (Dingwall)
Mr John Wilson (Corpach)

160